Poetic Imagination
in Black Africa

Poetic Imagination in Black Africa

Essays on African Poetry

Tanure Ojaide

CAROLINA ACADEMIC PRESS

Durham, North Carolina

Library of Congress Cataloging-in-Publication Data

Ojaide, Tanure,   1948–
    Poetic imagination in Black Africa : essays on African poetry / by
Tanure Ojaide.
    p.   cm.
    Includes bibliographical references and index.
    ISBN 0-89089-855-3
    1. African poetry—Black authors—History and Criticism.
2. Blacks—Africa—Intellectual life.   I. Title.
PL8010.4.036   1996
896—dc20   96-16122
                                                CIP

Carolina Academic Press
700 Kent Street
Durham, North Carolina 27701
Telephone (919) 489-7486
Fax (919) 493-5668

Printed in the United States of America

To my teachers and students

Contents

Foreword

This book is a collection of essays which from the beginning I conceived with the unifying objective of illuminating modern African poetry. Some of these essays have been published, others presented at conferences, and the rest recently written to complete the project. I have decided to start with "African Literature and Cultural Identity" to situate African literature generally, before specifically dealing with the poetry. This is followed by "The Way We Sing And Tell: Defining Modern African Poetic Aesthetics." One cannot judge "American football" by the rules of "British football!" Other essays deal with, among others, orality in modern African poetry, contemporary African poetry, new trends in modern African poetry, and African women's poetry. The essays are rounded up by the earliest-written "Poetic Imagination in Black Africa."

These essays are conceived as an alternative to Ivory Tower theorists of African poetry in particular and of African literature in general. Many critics of modern African poetry tend to employ theories spawned in Western academies to approach African literature no doubt with the belief that what applies to American or British literature also applies to any other literature. The essays here are based on the premise that theories and art are cultural products. Many of these foreign-spawned theories have made African writing and writers look ludicrous at best and inferior at worst. Do these theories help the reader to understand African literature? An emphatic No. My aim here is to explain the uniqueness of modern African poetry. I feel the right place to start is the available texts and they are many. Reading modern African poetry will lead to an understanding of certain features, which appear unique to it, compared to poetry from elsewhere in the world. Using whatever literary theory happens to be current in Europe and North America to interpret or judge African poetry is disingenuous. Also instead of imposing theories on modern African poetry, one could more reasonably theorize from the specifics of African poetry texts.

Literature is an art and a cultural product. Cultures differ in sensibility and response to reality. Literary aesthetics differ from culture to culture. I have always given the example to my students of three highly regarded art works: Mona Lisa, Benin Bronze Head, and Buddhist Sculpture. The European World hails Mona Lisa as the ultimate in art, as Africans the Benin Bronze Head, and Orientals Buddhist Sculpture. No artist is an airplant as (s)he is rooted in a specific space and time. The interaction of the individual with time and space will give birth to human experience. I thus feel uncomfortable when Westerners attempt to appropriate the universal. While the human is easier for me to accept than the universal, there is no doubt in my mind that cultural differences exist. My major aim in this book therefore is to identify modern African poetry.

While I accept cultural differences, it should not be mistaken that changes do not alter cultures. No culture in the modern world can remain in a pristine state. I can imagine Homi Bhabha jumping up and saying "And that's hybridity!" Culture is dynamic as it absorbs some things and discards others. A culture is capable of absorbing the bad from others and discarding some of its own good aspects. African culture has been this in relation to the Western culture in many ways.

Another premise of this book is that one can best understand the literature of a people from their total experience: historical, socio-cultural, political, economic, and other backgrounds. Art has a cultural role in Africa where it is traditionally functional. The artist has responsibilities, and certain dynamics relate the artist to his or her audience. The aesthetic indicators of an artist's culture should be highlighted to help interpret his or her work. It is possible for artists to differ from their tradition, but the poet comes out of a tradition.

Myself a poetry practitioner and a scholar of African literature, I tap on various experiences of African poetry. I am a double insider of African poetry, who happens to know Western, especially British and American, poetry. In my attempt to "define" African poetry, I make comparisons with the obvious "other." By describing the poetic imagination in black Africa, I hope to place modern African poetry in its proper place among world literatures.

The University of North Carolina at Charlotte
September 25, 1995

Acknowledgments

Some chapters of this book as stated in the foreword have appeared in article form in journals: "African Literature and Cultural Identity" in *African Studies Review*; "Musical Roots: the Rhythm of Modern African Poetry" in *Middle Atlantic Writers Association Journal*; "The Changing Voice of History: Contemporary African Poetry" in *Geneve-Afrique*; "New Trends in Modern African Poetry" in *Research in African Literatures*; "I Want to Be an Oracle: My Poetry and My Generation" in *World Literature Today*; and "Poetic Imagination in Black Africa" in *The Syracuse Scholar*. Grateful acknowledgments are made to all the journals in which these articles first appeared.

Poetic Imagination
in Black Africa

Modern African Literature and Cultural Identity

Modern African literature has gained recognition worldwide with such classics as Chinua Achebe's *Things Fall Apart*, Ngugi wa Thiongo's *Weep Not Child*, and Wole Soyinka's *Death and the King's Horseman*. This recognition was reinforced by Soyinka's winning of the Nobel Prize for Literature in 1986. Modern African literature is written in indigenous African languages and in European languages used in Africa. Written African literature is very new compared to the indigenous oral tradition of literature which has been there and is still very much alive. While there are literary works in Yoruba, Hausa, Zulu and Sotho, among others, this literature in African indigenous languages is hardly known outside its specific linguistic frontiers. Writers such as Mazisi Kunene, Ngugi wa Thiongo and the late Okot p'Bitek first wrote some of their works in African languages before translating them into English. Most African writers, however, write in English, French, and Portuguese. There is the Eurocentric temptation to see modern African literature written in these European languages as an extension of European literature. However, after modern imperialism, language alone cannot be the sole definer of a people's literature.

Defining African literature, Abiola Irele writes:

> The term 'Africa' appears to correspond to a geographical notion but we know that, in practical terms, it also takes in those areas of collective awareness that have been determined by ethnic, historical and sociological factors, all these factors, as they affect and express themselves in our literature, marking off for it a broad area of reference. Within this area of reference then, and related to certain aspects that are intrinsic to the literature, the problem of definition involves as well a consideration of aesthetic modes in their intimate correlation to the cultural and social structures which determine and define the expressive schemes of African peoples and societies (10).

This definition of literature takes note of place with its people and society having "aesthetic modes" and "cultural and social structures." Language is not the prime focus in this definition of literature, whose "essential force" is "its reference to the historical and experiential" (Irele 11). African writers create works "which are peculiarly African and yet set in the modern world" (Mbiti 228). It is this cultural distinctiveness that I intend to tackle in discussing modern African literature in English.

Ethical and Moral Nature of African Civilization

Traditionally, African literature is an informal evening fire-side school in which elders and parents teach the young ones ethics, morality, and the culture of the community. The inter-relatedness of literature and morality is demonstrated by various poetic traditions in Africa. An example is the Igbo *Mbari* tradition, a celebration through art of the world and the life lived in it. It is performed by the community on command by its presiding deity, the Earth goddess Ani. Ani "combined two formidable roles in the Igbo pantheon as fountain of creativity in the world and custodian of the moral order in human society. An abominable act is called *nso-ani*, taboo-to-Earth" (Achebe 1990, 167). Thus African literature is traditionally didactic. The writer in modern-day Africa has assumed the role of the conscience of the society, reminding readers and society of the high cultural ethos that must be upheld. Since the small communities have merged into states, writers now focus on nation-states; hence they produce many works of literature satirizing the corruption of modern governments. Almost all the works of Chinua Achebe, Wole Soyinka, and Ngugi wa Thiongo are criticisms of negative social and political practices. The aim of the criticisms is to change the transgressors of sociopolitical ethics and morality into positive agents in society.

Utilitarian Function of African Literature

There is, culturally speaking, no art for art's sake in Africa. Every literary work has a social function. Songs, prayers, praise chants, and abuse are placed at the service of the community. This utilitarian function of orature is imbibed by modern writers. Rites of passage are celebrated with poems. In *Idanre and Other Poems* Soyinka bases "Dedication: for Moremi" on the naming ceremony of his Yoruba people. The speaker-parent of the poem impresses upon the daughter the African cherished qualities of fertility, wealth, and longevity. For the child to live to be a worthy ancestor, the poet exhorts:

> Fruits then to your lips: haste to repay
> The debt of birth. Yield man-tides like the sea
> And ebbing, leave a meaning on the fossilled sands.   (25).

Ancestors are highly valued in traditional Africa and everybody lives to be a deserving one. In "For Georgette" in Christopher Okigbo's

Heavensgate, the birth of a child is symbolic of communal renewal and revitalization. In Achebe's *Anthills of the Savannah* there is also a naming ceremony of Ikem and Elewa's daughter. She is symbolic of hope for the future. Children are highly cherished in Africa as a means of immortalizing the race. The death of very old people is also celebrated as in Achebe's *Things Fall Apart*. Modern African literature is the repository of the cultural life of the people and is a major source of education for the young everywhere and for urban people who have lost touch with their roots.

Social Cohesion

The African writer has been nurtured in a society in which the sense of community is very strong. A cardinal point for understanding the African view of humankind is the belief that "I am, because we are; and since we are, therefore I am" (Mbiti 108–109). Literature in Africa has been and remains an affirmation of faith in one's cultural ideals. Social cohesiveness is very important to Africans because they believe that "the earliest act of civilization was...the establishment of a cooperative, interactive, human community." Kunene adds:

> The idea of integrating the artist's vision within a broad social experience becomes a normal and natural process that does not require rules for its application. Both the philosophic and artistic worlds fuse to produce a discipline that aims at affirming the social purpose of all expressions of human life. In short, the ideal of social solidarity is projected (xvi).

Modern African literature is very socialized. This literature is different from that which focuses on the individual. It is this communal spirit which informs the characterization and social analysis in Soyinka's *Interpreters*, Ngugi's *Petals of Blood*, and Achebe's *Anthills of the Savannah*. In each of these novels a group, rather than an individual, is emphasized. There is no single protagonist that overwhelms other characters. For instance, in *Anthills of the Savannah* it is the fate of the nation of Kangan that is at stake in the lives of Sam, Christopher Oriko, Ikem Oshodi, and Beatrice Okoh. Similarly in Achebe's *Things Fall Apart* and Soyinka's *Death and the King's Horseman*, the community can be said to be a protagonist struggling against Western intruders to maintain its cultural practices. The focus on society with its attendant social criticism in modern African literature is in the African tradition.

Defense of African Culture

African writers, in affirming their faith in their native culture, defend it against alien encroachment and prejudices. The Negritude writers asserted their Africanity to fight against colonial prejudices. Even though at times the poets might have romanticized the African past, their exaggerated portrayal is a weapon against cultural annihilation. Every African writer is a negritudinist in one way or another. One example of the defense of the indigenous culture against the invading Western one is expressed in Okigbo's *Heavensgate*. The contrast is clearly expressed in the use of negative images to describe alien culture and positive ones to describe the African way of life. John the Baptist is made ridiculous as he carries a "bowl of salt water" "preaching the gambit: / life without sin, / without life" (6). The alien imperialists, in trying to save people's souls, according to Okigbo, sowed the "fire-seeds" of destruction. Jadum may be half-demented but he expresses the African ethical viewpoint. He admonishes:

> Do not wander in speargrass,
> After the lights,
> Probing lairs in stockings,
> To roast
> The viper alive, with dog lying
> Upsidedown in the crooked passage...
>
> Do not listen at keyholes,
> After the lights,
> To smell from other rooms,
> After the lights   (8).

This is an affirmation of African religions which attempt to save lives rather than souls as alien Christianity is supposed to be doing.

In a similar way, Okot p'Bitek of Uganda in *Song of Lawino* imbues Lawino, the symbol of African cultural independence, with dignity, humility, respect, and authenticity. She is opposed to Clementine and Ocol who indiscriminately copy alien Western ways of life and so look absurd. Lawino assumes the royalty and courage of the bull and the beauty and gracefulness of the giraffe; but repulsive creatures such as the hyena, monkey, ostrich, and python represent the copied alien ways.

African writers, in asserting their cultural identity, condemn Western intervention as disruptive of the growth and development of African culture through colonialism. Cultural habits and practices change and the writers generally feel that there were and still are sufficient mechanisms and ample latitude for internal changes in African cultural life.

After all, culture is dynamic. As Achebe demonstrates in *Things Fall Apart*, such practices as the throwing away of twins, the *osu* caste system, human sacrifice, and exiling a person for inadvertent murder were already being questioned from within by Obierika and others. Africa did not need colonialists and the Christian religion to change. In Soyinka's *Death and the King's Horseman*, the dramatist's viewpoint suggests that the practice of the king's horseman accompanying him to the spirit world by ritual suicide was already failing and needed no colonial intervention to stop. The colonial officer's intervention resulted in a greater tragedy for the society in the waste of two lives in the place of one. Mazisi Kunene, the South African poet and scholar, has cautioned in *The Ancestors and the Sacred Mountain* against any group assuming ethical and moral superiority over others because of its material and technological advantages (xi). Material and technological advancement and ethical and moral advancement do not necessarily go together and are in fact antithetical in the experience of both Africa and Europe. As cultural standard-bearers of their people, African writers use literature to assert cultural independence.

African Mystical Life

Africans are generally a spiritually minded people. It can be said that "the whole psychic atmosphere of African village life is filled with belief in...mystical power" (Mbiti 197). It holds true also of city life. As a result of this, the supernatural plays an important part in African literature, especially in the drama and fiction. This belief in the supernatural is sometimes wrongly dismissed as superstition. The mystically minded African believes that not everything that happens in life can be explained rationally. There are ancestors, spirits, and gods influencing the affairs of the living. There are natural laws which when violated trigger punitive responses in the form of ailments from the spiritual world. Witches and wizards abound in societies to cause mainly mischief. Diviners and medicine-men also abound to ward off evil forces from individuals, families, and communities by recommending sacrifices.

The mystical nature of the African worldview is copiously reflected in modern African literature. Elechi Amadi in *The Concubine* writes of a beautiful lady who is dedicated to the gods and the man who marries her and incurs a fatal curse on himself. Zulu Sofola in *Wedlock of the Gods* deals with a similar theme.

Divinities proliferate in African literary works. Achebe's *Things Fall Apart* and *Arrow of God* portray the supremacy of Ani, the Earth goddess of the Igbo people. Any offence against the Earth goddess is punished seriously. For instance, when Okonkwo beats his wife during the

Week of Peace, he offends the goddess and is punished for it. Soyinka exploits the Yoruba pantheon in his poems, novels, and plays. "Idanre," the title poem of *Idanre and Other Poems*, is centered on Ogun, "God of Iron and metallurgy, Explorer, Artisan, Hunter, God of war, Guardian of the Road" (Soyinka 86). Ogun is the "septuple god." In the same poem there are references to Sango, god of lightning and electricity; Orunmila, the Sky-god and essence of wisdom; and Esu, god of chance and disruption. In *The Interpreters* Kola's sculpture of the Yoruba pantheon is a reflection of the mystical and spiritual lives of the characters of society.

The theme of reincarnation as of *abiku/ogbanje*, the wanderer-child, in the poetry of J. P. Clark and Soyinka and in Achebe's *Things Fall Apart* is a reflection of the beliefs of African people. Spirit possession, a mystical experience, has been exploited by dramatists and novelists. Achebe's traditional priestesses experience spirit possession. The mystical worldview that informs modern African literature is highly visible in the way gods and priests affect the course of things in society. Ritual with its accompanying solemn music and chants has been an asset to African drama and poetry in particular and literature in general.

Order and Justice

African writers have in various ways attempted to explain the African concept of order as opposed to the Western/colonial, which is equated with obeying man-made laws. Achebe, Ngugi, and Soyinka have all dealt with this theme. The colonialists in Achebe's *Things Fall Apart* and *Arrow of God* impose their laws on Africans, introduce Western courts and police, and forcibly jail those opposed to them. According to these foreigners, they are trying to maintain law and order. In traditional Africa there are no jails. Justice is done for the reconciliation of the affected parties, not to set them on parallel paths the rest of their lives. In traditional courts, reparations, restitutions, and settlements are made to the offended party, but the community or family makes sure that the two parties are reconciled. The justices of Umuofia—masquerades—in *Things Fall Apart* are good examples of traditional African dispensation of justice.

Order to Africans is perceived as natural and ritualistic to ensure harmony, the absence of which will bring calamity to the whole group. For this reason, an individual could be sacrificed to avoid a war, a plague, or any anticipated communal disaster. In other words, the individual can be sacrificed for the well-being of the community. Because of the spiritual nature of African society,

Most African peoples accept or acknowledge God as the final guardian of law and order and of the moral and ethical codes. Therefore the breaking of such order, whether by the individual or by a group, is ultimately an offence by the corporate body of society (Mbiti 206).

Wole Soyinka deals with the practice of individuals being used as their community's carriers in both *The Strong Breed* and *Death and the King's Horseman*. In *Mandela's Earth and Other Poems* there is the suggestion of the African nationalist leader being a sort of carrier for his black people because of his strong will and sense of sacrifice. Perhaps the best expressed clash of African and Western notions of law and order in African literature is found in Soyinka's *Death and the King's Horseman*. The Oyo people had a practice in which whenever the king died, his prime minister (horseman) ritually killed himself to accompany his master to the spirit world. This practice had been there from the beginning of the Oyo Kingdom and had continued to ensure stability in the state. Then came the turn of Elesin Oba in 1946 and, though vacillating, his death was stopped by the colonial administrator who detained him. Of course, the colonialists, who "have no regard for what they do not understand," called the practice suicide and a barbaric custom. However, Elesin's son Olunde, who had been pursuing medical studies in England, returned and killed himself in his father's place to save the family from shame. It was only after seeing his son's corpse and the irredeemable shame he had brought upon himself for doubly failing his duty that he strangled himself in detention. Where African law and order demanded an old man for the stability of the state, two lives were lost with the attendant tragic consequences. In this example, culture is used in modern African literature to question European/Western ignorance of other people's ways and to criticize the arrogant behavior which causes tragedy for others.

Land

Africans are bound mystically to their land. The land is sacred and dedicated to the ancestors and gods. Before a house is built or a farm started, there is libation to the earth. Of course, everybody is aware that it is the earth that receives one at the end of life. Land sustains the corporate existence of Africans, and families quarrel over a piece of land, sometimes with casualties.

Ngugi has made the relationship between people and their land the major focus in many of his works, especially in *Weep Not Child* and *Petals of Blood*. Land is so important in *Weep Not Child* that:

Any man who had land was considered rich. If a man had plenty of money, many motor cars, but no land, he could never be counted as

rich. A man who went with tattered clothes but had at least an acre
of red earth was better than the man with money (22).

It is in this light that the many African writers' concern with the impact
of land on characters and society can be better understood. Land own-
ership means wealth, stability, honor, and dignity. Lack of it means
poverty, rootlessness, and no dignity. The Gikuyu loss of land in colonial times was highly resented. Ngotho and Kamau among others work
as *shamba* boys on land which had previously belonged to their families. Land gave impetus to the Mau Mau insurrection against British
colonialism which ushered in Kenyan political independence. In *Petals
of Blood* the black exploiting group of Chui, Mzigo, and Kimeria appropriate other people's land. This is highly resented and eventually
leads to their being killed.

Land features in another manner in African literature. Land is sometimes identified with the traditional rural environment. In West African
and South African writings, the movement from rural to urban areas
causes a sense of alienation in the characters. As Mbiti puts it, the "de-
tachment from the land to which Africans are mystically bound, and
the thrust into situations where *corporate existence* has no meaning,
have produced dehumanized individuals in the mines, industry and
cities" (219). Alienation from the land is a major theme in African literature, more so than in Western literature. In Africa every day is Earth
Day, not one day in the year!

African Folklore

Folktales, proverbs, myths, and legends, all parts of the rich African
folklore, are very much alive and they infuse modern African literature
with motifs, themes, characters, and techniques. Ngugi draws a lot from
Gikuyu folklore in *The River Between*, *Weep Not Child* and *Petals of
Blood*. Jack Mapanje, the Malawian poet, draws much from native
folklore in *Of Chameleons and Gods*. He uses mythical characters to
criticize contemporary society. He admits that "Glory Be To Chingwe's
Hole" has an obscure reference to a Chewa myth:

> Do you remember Frog the carver carving Ebony Beauty?
> Do you remember Frog's pin on Ebony Beauty's head
> That brought Ebony to life? And when the Chief
> Heard of a beauty betrothed to Frog, whose dogs
> Beat up the bushes to claim Ebony for the Chief?
>
> Even when Fly alarmed Frog of the impending hounds
> Who cracked Fly's bones? Chingwe's Hole, woodpeckers

Once poised for vermillion strawberries merely
Watched fellow squirrels bundled up in sacks
Alive as your jaws gnawed at their brittle bones.   (44).

This myth is used to portray the selfishness and meanness of modern African rulers.

Many of the animals and plants in Africa evoke characteristics emanating from folklore. This cultural trait is reflected in characters which are more symbols (pejoratively called *types* in Western critical parlance) than just themselves. Ngugi's Matigari is a good example of the representational character common in African literature. The representational dimension derives from folktales. African dramatists in particular have exploited the trickster motif in their plays. As animals such as the tortoise and the hyena are not just animals but human representations, so are characters modeled on them representatives. Zulu Sofola's *Wizard of Law* and Soyinka's *The Trials of Brother Jero* are examples. Some of the most impressive anecdotes in Achebe's works are derived from Igbo folklore. The tortoise who suffers for his greed and cunning recurs in many African novels and plays.

Though allusions to folklore may be obscure to outsiders, they give a certain profundity to the literature. Ibrahim Tala rightly observes that in Africa

> new writers incorporate oral literature in their writing to give a flavour of authenticity to their works and to show as modern Africans [they] are conscious of a rich source of literary inspiration. They include oral tradition to link their past with their present experience (as a group), to localize the content of their works, to educate fellow Africans and give them confidence in their cultural heritage and to enlighten outsiders and help them get rid of the false impression about African cultures acquired from years of cultural misrepresentation (95–96).

Traditional African literary forms and techniques have been adopted by modern writers. In drama the storyteller features in plays by Soyinka, Ola Rotimi, and Femi Osofisan. Ngugi's *Devil on the Cross* is told by a Gicaandi Player. African poetry has distinctly traditional African rhythms. In many cases, the poet superimposes European words on an existing musical composition. As I have written elsewhere,

> There are certain poetic forms with innate generic rhythms. Africans thus writing dirges, abuse songs, praise chants, odes, and other poetic forms instinctively fall back on traditional African rhythms associated with the forms they want to use (1989, 9).

Kofi Awoonor's "Songs of Sorrow" reflects the slow mournful rhythm of the Ewe dirge:

Dzogbese Lisa has treated me thus
It has led me among the sharps of the forest
Returning is not possible
And going forward is a great difficulty
The affairs of this world are like the chameleon faeces
Into which I have stepped
When I clean it cannot go.

I am on the world's extreme corner,
I am not sitting in the row with the eminent
But those who are lucky
Sit in the middle and forget
I am on the world's extreme corner
I can only go beyond and forget.   (Moore and Beier 98).

The Yoruba-speaking poets have absorbed the *ijala* and *oriki* chant rhythms of their people. In "Muhammad Ali at the Ringside, 1985" Soyinka chants:

Black tarantula whose antics hypnotize the foe!
Butterfly sideslipping death from rocket probes.
Bee whose sting, unsheathed, picks the teeth
Of the raging hippopotamus, then fans
The jaw's convergence with its flighty wings.
Needle that threads the snapping fangs
Of crocodiles, knots the tusks of elephants
On rampage. Cricket that claps and chirrups
Round the flailing horn of the rhinoceros,
Then shuffles, does a bugalloo, tap-dances on its tip.
Space that yields, then drowns the intruder
In showers of sparks—oh Ali! Ali!
Esu with faces turned to all four compass points
Astride a weather vane; they sought to trap him,
Slapped the wind each time.   (*Mandela's Earth*, 48).

Similarly, Niyi Osundare in *The Eye of the Earth* sings the Earth's praise in *oriki* rhythms. Though not of Yoruba origin, but benefiting from his studies and working experience in Ibadan, Christopher Okigbo uses incantatory rhythms to sing the praise of W.B. Yeats in "Lament of the Masks:"

THEY THOUGHT you would stop pursuing the white elephant
They thought you would stop pursuing the white elephant
But you pursued the white elephant without turning back—
You who charmed the white elephant with your magic flute

You who trapped the white elephant like a common rabbit
You who sent the white elephant tumbling into your net—
And stripped him of his horns, and made them your own—
You who fashioned his horns into ivory trumpets—
They put you into the eaves thatch
You split the thatch
They poured you into an iron mould
You burst the mould...   (Maxwell and Bushrui xiv).

This form of repetition unique in *ijala*, the hunter's chant, gives a distinctive African flavor to the rhythm of modern African poetry. Traditional forms and rhythms affect its diction, prosody, syntax, and other linguistic aspects.

African writers are students of their folklore. Soyinka researched into Yoruba oral drama between 1959 and 1961. Kofi Awoonor collected and translated Ewe dirges in a book titled *Guardians of the Sacred Word*. Clark worked on the Ozidi saga of the Ijo people. Kofi Anyidoho is a trained folklorist. Mapanje researched into Chewa oral literature. Zainab Alkali studied Bura folklore. I have worked on the oral literature of the Urhobo people and the songs and epics of northeastern Nigeria. This study of folklore or involvement in its preservation is a form of professional apprenticeship for writers and the knowledge gained gives one the confidence to operate from the cultural milieu.

African Time and Space in Literary Form and Vision

Traditional African concepts of time and space have their impact on literary form and vision. Time is seen not only as lineal but cyclical. Thus death is the beginning of a spiritual existence, and birth into this world is the end of one stage of existence. While the impact of this concept is strong in the *abiku* poems of both Soyinka and Clark and in the themes of reincarnation in the works of many writers, there is a subtle manifestation of the concept of time and space in the literary form. The refrain of traditional songs is a manifestation of this concept on a creative plane. In many poems, especially those of Mazisi Kunene, Okot p'Bitek, Kofi Awoonor, and Wole Soyinka, the beginning and end are connected to show a sense of continuity in the cyclical nature of things. In the novel, this break with lineal time could be problematic to outsiders who, for instance, cannot see the African time movement in works like Soyinka's *Interpreters* and Achebe's *Anthills of the Savannah*. These works are not static but have a certain movement which, while not denying a forward thrust, comes and goes in a continuing flux.

The breath-space of oral literature has its influence on modern African poetry. In the poetry of p'Bitek, Awoonor, Okigbo, Anyidoho, Osundare, and many others, the poetic line approximates a breath-space. This has generally given rise to long lines on the page, rather than the five-foot iambic line of English poetry. African people's culture is so strong that when they change their medium of artistic expression from oral to written, their creative products still bear their deep-rooted response to reality. African concepts of time and space inevitably form part of the "literary" aesthetics.

The Language of African Literature

The language of modern African literature whether written in English, French, or Portuguese is peculiarly African. It is informed by African languages with their proverbs, axioms, rhythms, and oratorical structures. I have already illustrated the transplanting of African rhythms into modern poetry. The tonal African languages have trained the ears of modern African poets to retain and use incantatory rhythms that iambic English and alexandrine French do not neutralize. As wisdom is highly appreciated in African societies and as "proverbs are the palm-oil with which words are eaten" (Achebe 1958, 5), oratory is an integral part of African literature. African literature carries proverbs, symbols, and folkloric connotations that are peculiar to the land. Thus the writer may be writing in English, but the words have different symbolic meaning than they have in mainstream English—if there is such a thing nowadays! Those lines from Awoonor's "Songs of Sorrow" come to mind again. When the speaker of the poem says "When I clean it cannot go," it has meaning to the African sharing the same linguistic base but may look quaint to other users of English. Similarly, "I can only go beyond and forget" expresses the speaker's desire to die and be relieved of his earthly suffering. Plants and animals like the *iroko* tree, the spider, tortoise, hyena, bull, and giraffe, among others, have symbolic meaning which African folklore has given them. In modern African literature the European languages used have been enriched by local color.

Universality

Unique as African literature is because of the culture it carries, many writers attempt to universalize the cultural experience. Soyinka has attempted this in his poetry, fiction, and drama. In his creative works and in *Myth, Literature and the African World,* Soyinka sees Yoruba gods as having Greek parallels. Ogun is likened to both Apollo and Dionysus, registering the Yoruba god's duality as creator and destroyer. In

Season of Anomy, Ofeyi is modeled on Orpheus while Iridise is modeled on Euridice and both characters in the novel are involved in a quest as their Greek counterparts were in classical literature. Jack Mapanje in a note of explanation says his poem "Glory Be To Chingwe's Hole" has an obscure reference to a myth, the "Chewa version of the Greek myth of Pygmalion" (77). Jared Angira of Kenya, Syl Cheney-Coker of Sierra Leone, and Lenrie Peters of The Gambia use classical allusions in their poems to extend their experiences beyond themselves as individuals and make these experiences timeless human ones. Archetypal and cross-cultural images and symbols relate African literature to other literatures of the world. For instance, in the poems of Ewe/Ghanaian Kofi Awoonor and Ijo/Nigerian J.P. Clark, there are references to the belief, also expressed in Greek classical literature, in the ferryman or boatman of death who comes to take away the dead across the sea to the spirit world. When African writers consciously or unconsciously use archetypal images, they validate and universalize the African experience. At the bottom of things, all peoples whether in Africa, the Americas, Asia or Europe are human. Though the African world is unique, "it possesses...in common with other cultures the virtues of complementarity" (Soyinka 1976, xii). In an increasingly cosmopolitan world, African writers borrow the relevant from other traditions. That is why, despite their uniqueness, they resemble others in some ways.

Conclusion

The indigenous culture has functioned effectively in modern African literature by giving it not only deep and solid roots but a concrete and relevant background and setting. The culture provides the literature with allusions, images and symbols, aesthetic direction and a moral and ethical imperative. African literature has distinguished itself in spite of colonial and neocolonial onslaughts on the native culture. The African culture in its material dimension has been used in literature to disabuse minds about colonialism and its justification. The ethically rich culture has enhanced the works of writers who see themselves as having the social role of cleansing the society. New novels, poems, and plays are modeled on folkloric forms and techniques and these works have demonstrated the affirmation of faith by different generations of African writers in their cultural heritage.

African literature is suffused with cultural traits. Modern drama is characterized by rituals, the supernatural, spirit possession, and a language enriched by proverbs. Fiction has many folkloric anecdotes and concentrates on the direction of the entire society, the land, and being in harmony with the environment. Poetry absorbs qualities of traditional oratory, ritual, incantatory rhythms, and symbolic animal and plant imagery originating from folklore. All three major genres—poetry, drama, and fiction—have gained tremendously from the oral tradition of African literature which when transferred to writing still retains its vibrant, live, audience-conscious, and concrete nature.

Modern African literature informed by African culture is utilitarian, more socialized than based on the individual psychology; it is community-oriented and didactic for ethical and moral instruction. It draws on the beliefs, worldview, and folkloric heritage of African people. Though written in European languages, modern African literature comes out distinctly African.

References

Achebe, Chinua. *Things Fall Apart*. London: Heinemann, 1958.

———. *Arrow of God.* London: Heinemann, 1964.

———. *Anthills of the Savannah*. London: Heinemann, 1987.

———. "Literature of Celebration." *West Africa*, 5–11 February, 1990; 167.

Alkali, Zainab. *The Stillborn*. Harlow/Lagos: Longman, 1984.

Amadi, Elechi. *The Concubine*. London: Heinemann, 1964.

Angira, Jared. *Cascades*. London: Longman, 1979.

Anyidoho, Kofi. *A Harvest of Our Dreams*. London: Heinemann, 1984.

———. *Earthchild*. Accra: WOELI, 1985.

Awoonor, Kofi, ed. *Guardians of the Sacred Word*. New York: NOK, 1974.

———. *Until the Morning After*. Greenfield Center, New York: Greenfield Review Press, 1987.

Cheney-Coker, Syl. *The Graveyard Also Has Teeth*. London: Heinemann, 1980.

Clark, J.P. *Ozidi*. Ibadan: Oxford UP, 1967.

———. *A Decade of Tongues*. London: Longman, 1981.

Irele, Abiola. *The African Experience in Literature and Ideology*. London: Heinemann, 1981.

Kunene, Mazisi. *The Ancestors and the Sacred Mountain*. London: Heinemann, 1982.

Mapanje, Jack. *Of Chameleons and Gods*. London: Heinemann, 1981.

Maxwell, D. F. S. and S.B. Bushrui, eds. *W.B. Yeats: 1865–1965 Centenary Essays*. Ibadan: Ibadan UP, 1965.

Mbiti, John S. *African Religions and Philosophy*. London: Heinemann, 1969.

Moore, Gerald and Ulli Beier, eds. *Modern Poetry from Africa*. Harmondsworth: Penguin, 1967.

Ngugi, wa Thiongo. *Weep Not Child*. London: Heinemann, 1964.

———. *The River Between*. London: Heinemann, 1965.

———. *Petals of Blood*. London: Heinemann, 1977.

———. *Devil on the Cross*. London: Heinemann, 1980.

———. *Matigari*. Oxford: Heinemann, 1989.

Ojaide, Tanure. "Poetic Imagination in Black Africa," *The Syracuse Scholar* (Spring 1983): 83–90.

———. *Labyrinths of the Delta*. Greenfield Center, New York: Greenfield Review Press, 1986.

———. *The Eagle's Vision*. Detroit: Lotus, 1987.

———. *The Endless Song*. Lagos: Malthouse, 1989.

———. *The Fate of Vultures and Other Poems*. Lagos: Malthouse, 1990.

———. *The Blood of Peace*. Oxford: Heinemann, 1991.

———. "Musical Roots: The Rhythm of Modern African Poetry," *Middle-Atlantic Writers Association Review*, vol. 7, no. 2 (December 1992).

Okigbo, Christopher. *Labyrinths*. London: Heinemann, 1971.

Osofisan, Femi. *Another Raft*. Lagos: Malthouse, 1988.

Osundare, Niyi. *Songs of the Marketplace*. Ibadan: New Horn, 1983.

———. *The Eye of the Earth*. Ibadan: Heinemann Nigeria Ltd, 1986.

———. *Moonsongs*. Ibadan: Spectrum, 1988.

———. *Waiting Laughters*. Lagos: Malthouse, 1990.

p'Bitek, Okot. *Song of Lawino*. Nairobi: East Africa Publ. House, 1966.

Peters, Lenrie. *Selected Poetry*. London: Heinemann, 1981

Rotimi, Ola. *The Gods Are Not To Blame*. London: Oxford UP, 1971.

Sofola, Zulu. *Wedlock of the Gods*. London: Evans, 1973.

———. *The Wizard of Law*. Ibadan: Evans, 1975.

Soyinka, Wole. *Idanre and Other Poems*. London: Eyre Methuen, 1967.

———. *The Interpreters*. London: Heinemann, 1970.

———. *Season of Anomy*. London: Rex Collings, 1973.

———. *Collected Plays I*. London: Oxford UP, 1973.

———. *Collected Plays II*. London: Oxford UP, 1974.

———. *Death and the King's Horseman*. London: Eyre Methuen, 1975.

———. *Myth, Literature and the African World*. London: Cambridge UP, 1976.

———. *Mandela's Earth and Other Poems*. New York: Random House, 1989.

Tala, Ibrahim Kashim. *An Introduction to Cameroun Oral Literature*. Yaounde: SOPECAM, 1984.

2

The Way We Sing and Tell: Defining Modern African Poetic Aesthetics

The griot always has a weakness for music, for music is the griot's soul.

> —Mamadou Kouyate, *Sundiata*

The aesthetics of any art form tend to be conditioned by the total experience of the people who practice it. The people's experience involves their culture and history. This aesthetic conditioning is expected since that very art is a product of a specific culture. A people who have had unique historical experiences focus the themes of their art works on what gives them an affirmation of their lives. Africans who had been enslaved and colonized are bound to use their art as a form of struggle against oppression and exploitation. As Addison Gayle puts it, Western aesthetic "aims to evaluate the work of art in terms of *its* beauty and not in terms of the transformation from ugliness to beauty that the work of art demands from its audience" in African societies (xxiii). In other words, a people's culture and history help to determine their aesthetic responses.

In light of Gayle's argument, the de-Westernization of African peoples lies at the heart of African poetic aesthetics as African poets use African gods and other cultural icons as images to express their peculiar experiences and affirm their Africanness. African poetic aesthetic advocates functional art, not art for art's sake. This means that the content (with its attendant didacticism) rather than the formal features per se of a poem weighs more in the minds of both artists and audience in evaluating artistic creations. The edifying aspect of the poem is crucial to its success or failure.

Aesthetic relates to "a system of isolating the artistic works of black people which reflect the special character and imperatives of black experience" (Gayle 9). African poetic aesthetics therefore involve the distinctive styles and rhythms that convey the African experience.

Critical Absurdities

Many literary critics, by not both recognizing and acknowledging its cultural background, tend to approach African poetry as if it is an extension of European literature. This tendency has led to absurdities of criticism. There were the critics of the late 1950s and early 1960s such as Gerald Moore and Ulli Beier who used Western critical canons to approach African literature. They highly rated African poets who used Western modernist techniques of fragmentation, intellectual allusion, and obscurity. This appears to have encouraged "obscurantist poets" like Wole Soyinka and Okigbo in their early creative careers. Chinweizu scorns the view "that for African poetry to acquire the obscurantist aims and deracinated habits of the Hopkinsian strand of euromodernist poetry constitutes progress..." (210).

There have also been the structuralists, deconstructionists, modernists, postmodernists, and postcolonialists. Sunday Anozie's *Conch* illustrates some of the absurdities that arise from rigidly using Western/European critical theories in approaching African poetry. In recent times (at the University of Calabar Literature Conference in 1991), Anozie has acknowledged that an African critical canon, rather than the Western, should be used to judge African creative works.

At the time of the critical onslaught on African writing, there were staunch defenders. Stanley Macebuh saw the so-called weaknesses of African literature as some of its strengths. He writes:

> Critics have claimed, for instance, that some of our contemporary writers tend to produce 'structureless' fictions and poems; that they are not often given to deep psychological analysis of the roots of personality; that they tend sometimes to be ponderously didactic; and they are rather incompetent pornographers; that their occasional excursions into existentialist thought are often pitifully mediocre; that they often show little respect for the austere and age-old distinctions between comedy and tragedy. The catalogue of their sins is virtually infinite. And yet, odd as it may at first seem, it is these very 'sins', when consciously committed, that constitute the most significant grounds for their claim to Africanness in art (21).

A recognition of the "Africanness" of African poetry is absolutely necessary for its critical evaluation.

African Psyche

Though modern written African literature is a product of European colonization and in its early stages was influenced by European and

American literary works, that relationship has become increasingly superficial. In modern African poetry, there is a psychic underlayer of Africanity, which distinguishes it from poetry elsewhere in the world. This psychic mark manifests itself in the aesthetics which govern the creative process and artistic product in African culture. Despite diversity in Africa, there are cultural affinities, especially in sub-Saharan Africa, which distinguish the continent.

In these days of postcoloniality and multiculturalism, literary critics of African literature in general and of the poetry in particular need to be cautious before using theories of specific cultures and literatures in approaching literatures of other peoples. The cultural factor in definitions of aesthetics in general and poetic aesthetics in particular is very important. Cultural differentiation is necessary to understand the plurality of the globe rather than taking the Western as universal.

Defining African poetic aesthetics would make critics assess the quality and other aspects of modern African poetry by the rules of its creation. What would it look like if rules of American football are used to judge British football, also called soccer? Certain crucial questions need to be asked and answered. For example, what are the organizing principles of African poetry in traditional and modern times? What impact has a culture of oral poetry performance on its written poetry? What effects are songs/poems expected to have on the audience/listeners? What gives pleasure in African oral and written poetry? What are expectations of audience of the poet and the poet of the audience? Above all, is taste socio-culturally determined? These are necessary questions to ask so as to find new and relevant criteria to use in assessing modern African poetry rather than using Western critical canons and any new theories spawned in American and European academies to judge poets of a different cultural and therefore aesthetic background.

The Cultural Imperative

While not subscribing to an essentialist view of African poetry, apparently there are unique qualities in the African poetic tradition. There are cultural, not universal, aesthetic traditions which inform all creative arts, including poetry. Sensibility and sensitivity are culturally defined as attitudes to other human beings, animals such as cats and dogs, and plants vary. For instance, Westerners seem to accept that the dog is man's best friend. However, most Africans would likely see the Supreme God as man's best friend, if not the other human. I use the term *aesthetic* here in a very wide sense to mean pleasurable and valuable taste. The aesthetics of any culture like the culture itself are never fixed as they change from internal and external pressures and influences.

I am aware of some recent studies that in the postcolonial wave in the Western academy tend to question whether there is an "African" of anything. Such critics do not question whether there is a Western civilization! Harold Bloom, for instance, understands the cultural and historical experience, hence he writes *The Western Canon: Books and Schools of the Ages*. Long ago F.R. Leavis has this in mind in *The Great Tradition*. Since to clearly define the self implies knowing the other, I will as I discuss African poetic aesthetics occasionally refer to the Western (Euro-American) poetic aesthetics.

Functional Art

Western and Eurocentric critics of African literature are quick to say that the literature is too didactic and political. It is necessary to study African poetic aesthetics to understand the fluid relationship between audience and artist and what they expect of the other in a tradition of collective participation. Knowing that the aesthetic value of an African artwork is based on the functional or symbolic aspects of the work (Warren and Andrews 10) is relevant to countering the Western critical attitude. The functionality of African art is emphasized again and again as in Molefi Asante:

> Thus the African sees the discourse as the creative manifestation of what is *called to be*. That which is *called to be*, because of the mores and values of the society, becomes the created thing; and the artist, or speaker, satisfies the demands of the society by calling into being that which is functional. Functionality, in this case, refers to the object (sculpture, music, poem, dance, speech) that possesses a meaning within the communicator's and audience's world view; a meaning that is constructed from the social, political, and religious moments in the society's history (64).

African art is not just meant to be beautiful alone but to be of value to the community. The value of a song or chant is articulated through figurative language and exuberance of diction.

Performance principles and didacticism are some of the strongest factors that define African poetic aesthetics. African poets expect to entertain and educate their readers. Cultural conditioning which gives rise to these two factors is an important background to the study of the poetic aesthetics in Africa. Cultural theory and reader-response by their very nature, if objectively applied, reinforce the performance and didacticism that form the fabric of the poetic aesthetics in Africa.

Oral Tradition of Modern African Poetry

Modern African poetry originating from colonial times and initially indebted to the European world poetry is governed by traditional African aesthetics. As has become apparent, modern African literature is written literature with an oral flavor. In other words, though written, the literature still carries traditional African oral rhetorical qualities. Abiola Irele in defining African literature asks for "a consideration of aesthetic modes in their intimate correlation to the cultural and social structures which determine and define the expressive schemes of African peoples and societies" (10). The "aesthetic modes" which define "the expressive schemes" of modern African poetry are embedded in the African tradition. Thus modern African poetry though written has the substructure of orature.

The orality of modern African poetry goes beyond formal and stylistic principles to involve content and meaning. Many modern African poets such as Soyinka, Awoonor, p'Bitek, and Clark-Bekederemo have immersed themselves in their indigenous poetic traditions, which they have either inherited or studied. Most traditional African songs/poems are composed for specific events and therefore relate some ideas. The impact of the meaning of the song is always a primary consideration. The traditional African poet is generally a communicator of ideas in a musical way. Among the Urhobo people of Nigeria, for instance, *udje* songs and dirges are composed for content and meaning, hence the *ororile*, poet-composer, makes the poem which is then sung by the *obo-ile*, cantor. In other words, while in American and British poetry, musicality can be in-built at the expense of meaning in the rhymes and other figures of sound such as alliteration and assonance, in traditional African poetry musicality is not expected to be in-built in the verbal structure. Rather it is an addition, an ornament, left for the falsetto voice to intone. The creative mind and the voice have their separate roles even though they are allies, because poetry in the African tradition does not end with only composition but includes its delivery. The emphasis is thus on the meaning rather than the musicality of words.

Many modern African poets have naturally imbibed these traditional oral literary qualities and write to communicate ideas. To Chinweizu, a "poem cannot just *be*, it must also mean" (166). Apart from early modern African poets and a few others who tried rhymes and in-built musicality at the beginning of their careers, most modern African poets use free verse to be more in tune with their aesthetic tradition. Christopher Okigbo is an example of such poets who started with the European poetic musicality in his *Heavensgate* and ended interestingly with an incantatory African voice in *Path of Thunder*. Soyinka's *Idanre* has excessive alliterations, but his *Mandela's Earth* sheds that euromodernist tendency. Niyi Osundare's use of alliteration in *Moonsongs* should be seen as an exception to the overwhelming lack of emphasis on English musical sounds in most African poets.

In most traditional African songs, voice, and not words, imposes rhyme because of the tonality of the languages. In Urhobo, the singer/poet/performer can always end a breath-space, a line equivalent, with a vowel such as a drawn-out *o-o-o* or *e-e-e*. Sound may be important in traditional and modern African poetry, but musicality is derived from other features which have more to do with performance. Rhyme may not be a favourite technique of mature African poets (it also smacks of colonialism!), but there is the propensity to exploit the tonality of words. Politicians such as S.L. Akintola, K.O. Mbadiwe, and Nnamdi Azikiwe were known at the peak of their political careers in Nigeria for exploiting the resources of English from their tonal background.

Modern African poets, especially those from Ghana such as Atukwei Okai and Kojo Laing, mix up English and Ghanaian words to enhance the sound value of their poetry. In "I am the freshly dead husband," Laing speaks of his "popylonkwe" still alive, a "supertobolo girlfriend," and adjusting "your duku in the mirror" (34–5). Much of *Godhorse* resounds with this exploitation of the tonality of African words to communicate ideas with irony and humor.

Content and Didacticism

The didactic consideration in African poetic aesthetics gives a pattern of story-telling in modern African poetry. It is not that in other cultures poets do not tell stories. However, the sense of urgency to make a statement, to instruct ethically and morally, and to entertain makes most African poets relate experiences through stories. The more indebted the poets are to oral tradition, the more common this narrative feature of modern African poetry. Okot p'Bitek, Mazisi Kunene, Taban Lo Liyong, and Kofi Anyidoho, among many others, tell stories in their poems. Lo Liyong's *The Cows of Shambat* illustrates this narrative trait of many African poets. The Rwachkaro poems in particular tell the story of a character. This is a very good technique as the poet without using the conventional ballad form succeeds in drawing the attention of the reader. Steve Chimombo's *Napolo and the Python* is also very narrative, drawing much from the oral tradition to describe the encounter between Mbona and Mlauli. There is constant alternation of dialogue and narration as modern African poets "sing" their "tales." This aesthetic aspect helps to make the poetry dynamic rather than static. There is movement on the page and this itself reinforces the dramatic nature of African poetry. Reading through, for instance, Kunene's *Ancestors and the Sacred Mountain* is like going through a collection of tales that reinforce his view of Africa's rich ethical heritage.

Most modern African poets see themselves as producing artistic works which will help to edify their very societies. As Odun Balogun puts it, "African Art is a socially committed Art" (19). Balogun also talks of the "thematic focus" in African literature as a result of the artists' didacticism. There was the time when African poets saw themselves as defenders of African culture against Western denigration of the African. In much of modern African poetry, there has been a shift from the white/black conflict to a black/black conflict. In modern African poetry as in traditional African songs, there is the focus on current sociopolitical issues that affect the poet's people. The criticism of political leadership and the "ranging on the side of the masses" are major concerns in contemporary African poetry. Such concerns could be seen in the Western canon defined by Harold Bloom as "extraliterary."

The need to convey meaning naturally affects the poetic style. The attempt in African poetry is aimed at comprehension on many levels. This means that the poet uses diction that reflects a measure of the knowledge of his or her audience. The topical allusions are supposed to be understood by members of the society.

The Power of the Word

Traditional concepts of poetry such as oratory and performance, key aesthetic considerations, help to define modern African poetry. As Chinua Achebe's *Things Fall Apart* and *Arrow of God* show, Africans traditionally value oratory in verbal communication. The place of *otota*/spokesperson is highly converted among Urhobo and other African peoples. Who presents and responds to issues on behalf of a group is an orator who weaves words artistically to open up avenues and soften difficult issues. The frequent use of proverbs, anecdotes, axioms, and other wise sayings by African poets confirms the broad poetic repertory of the tradition.

In traditional as well as modern Africa, it is not the verse that makes the poem. Apart from France with a strong tradition of prose poetry, the poem in the West seems synonymous with verse. Poetry is the quality of word use to effectively meet its aim in an intellectually pleasing way. This tradition exists in modern African poetry. In the African song or chant, there is a very thin or rather invisible line between prose and poetry. Most African traditional songs could be seen as prose poetry. African orature does not departmentalize literature into poetry, prose, and drama but just language use by the performer. How many times in contemporary American poetry do we find words that have to do with certain colors and sounds such as "white," "turquoise," and "hummingbird," as if using them means being poetic? There is the emphasis on images which touch all the senses in Western poetry, but as will be touched later African images are drawn more from the fauna and flora of the poet's environment.

Examples of the use of language rooted in the indigenous African culture are copious. In fact, the use of African culture-derived tropes could be said to be a strong determining factor of modern African poetry. Kofi Awoonor, Kofi Anyidoho, Wole Soyinka, Niyi Osundare, J.P. Clark, Okot p'Bitek, and Taban lo Liyong, among others, dexterously employ African tropes to give an authentic African touch to the experiences they articulate.

Lyricism

The lyricism of modern African poetry is an offshoot of traditional songs and tales. As Macebuh puts it:

> Traditional African narrative tends to be fluid, repetitious, incantatory, even 'structureless,' but far from being 'formless,' it seeks indeed to recapture, through...direct mimesis, the oceanic infinitude and the interpenetration of things, in the universe (qtd. in Balogun 22).

Much as there is form whether it is *udje, ijala, oriki, izibongo,* or something else, there remains a certain fluidity in modern African poetry. This lyricism is achieved through various devices of repetition. J.P. Clark in *A Reed in the Tide* and *Casualties* illustrates the general lyricism of modern African poetry. The poet's Niger Delta roots and the civil war atmosphere particularly make *Casualties* highly lyrical.

Performance

The inherited performance quality of oral poetry has bearing on the aesthetic composition of modern African poetry. As I have mentioned of the Urhobo *udje* practice, the poet and cantor, composer and performer, may not necessarily be the same person but are likely to be. Even when they are different, they are mindful of the other's presence. In other words, verbal composition and performance are intricately related. Since the modern poet is more likely to perform his/her own poetry, these performance qualities are built into the poem. The story told in a poem engenders its own dramatics. Much extemporization is still a part of written African poetry as songs or refrains are extended in poetry readings. The relationship between audience and performer which is controlled in the West is more spontaneous in Africa. Modern African poets attempt to involve their audience, and this also influences the compositional process. Readings from, among others, Femi Osofisan's *Dream-Seeker on Divining Chain*, Niyi Osundare's *Eye of the Earth*, and Tanure Ojaide's *Blood of Peace* have poems with refrains that involve the audience.

There is an inherent delight in action in both traditional and modern African poetry. The poetry dramatizes action. As often occurs in the African epic, there is a "transactional approach." The poet asks rhetorical questions to show that the poet is not a lone actor but one involved in a dialogic event. The rhetorical questions as in Taban lo Liyong in part engage the audience/reader. Many formulaic expressions, dramatics, markers, additives, and improvisation promote the liveliness of the poetic art.

Repetition

The variety of repetition in modern African poetry is a carry-over from the oral tradition. The use of the chorus/refrain/call-and-response affords the lead singer opportunity to relax, inhale and exhale, and at the same time have a moment to recapture from memory what is ahead. Repetition, especially in the form of refrain, is commonly used by African poets of both the older and the younger generations. This is almost universal and every established African poet offers many examples. The point needs to be made though that some poets like Christopher Okigbo use repetition to make music, while others like Lo Liyong to emphasize. But in either case, repetition generates monotonous rhythm. In African music, repetition involves regularity of beat with occasional and improvised variations. Regularity of beat is pleasing to the ear and functions doubly as both mnemonic and musical devices.

An often ignored type of repetition in modern African poetry is the structural. This derives from grammatical parallelism and antithetical balancing. An example appears in Anyidoho's *Earthchild*:

> Monkey was caught in a trap
> Consider the fate of Rat
> Lizard has lost his tail
> What may become of Fox?
> Chameleon was found out
> Old Frog got drowned last night
> And Cock has lost his voice   (102).

There is antithetical balance in "Yesterday was someone's day / Today for someone else" (Anyidoho 103). Parallelism helps to impose a formal order on the poems which could be seen at first sight as "free" verse.

The Native Accent

The tonality of African indigenous languages cannot be overemphasized. Since orality is still much alive in Africa, even when secondary, the poetic voice is more demonstrative than the Euro-American poetic voice. Many Africans speak and write English, French, and Portuguese from the tonal standpoint of their own languages. As I wrote elsewhere, some African poets impose the foreign languages they write on pre-existing indigenous poetic/musical forms (Ojaide 92:67). The example of the song in the Urhobo folktale of the tortoise in *Labyrinths of the Delta* tells the depth of the aesthetic conditioning of modern African poets. In the book's title poem the poet in relating the colonial experience of the Delta people of Nigeria compares the European colonialists to the tortoise who is a trickster and great cheat. This segment of the poem is virtually a recast of the song in the folktale:

> Turn the tortoise back, O Waters,
> Bring him back
> Spare him mishap on the way
> Bring him back to me;
> He broke not only my hands
> But also my legs and ribs;
> Bring him back to me
> Spare him mishap on the way here
> And let the villain taste
> What he inflicted on me
> From my own hands   (26).

Yoruba-speaking poets like Wole Soyinka, Femi Osofisan, and Niyi Osundare have modelled many of their poems on *ijala* and *oriki* rhythms. Kofi Anyidoho's "Song" is "in part a translation of ... an original Ewe song by one of the poet-cantors of the *Haikot tu* Drum of my birthplace, Wheta" (*Earthchild*, 47). Similarly, Okigbo's later poems, especially the "elegies," display an orality modelled on indigenous African rather than English rhythms.

Observing Africans and Westerners read their poetry tells a lot about Africa's demonstrativeness. "Poetry reading" is common in American literary circles. In Africa, writers perform their work.

Modern Africans aware of their oral tradition and also of their audience's expectation of a live performance write their poems in a "speaking" voice. The modern African poet internally vocalizes lines as the traditional performer did and still does with breath-space. The very form of the poem depends on the performance model the poet instinctively chooses. If the poem is a chant, the lines are usually long as the breath-space is stretched to its limits. However, if the poem is a praise or curse, the lines are likely to be short to give emphasis to every word. In the United States the performance poets as in the San Francisco/Bay area are outside the mainstream of American poets.

Art as a Social Form

The socio-cultural background of a people also affects their aesthetic response. Poetry in traditional Africa is a public art in the sense that the thematic focus is on ideas which affect society and the human. Satirization of human vices like witchcraft, greed, inhumanity, and others was intended to bring the deviants into line so as to uphold the social ethos. Modern African poets criticize the political corruption in their respective societies. It appears to me that African poets dwell more on public experiences than private and have been more successful with the former. The frequent use of "we" shows that the poet's role is the public one of defending communal values. While there are songs/poems in traditional society of self-lamentation and exhortation, individual artists seem to have seen themselves more as serving the community rather than themselves. This again explains the didactic nature of the African aesthetic consideration. The poet is traditionally committed to the society that gave birth to him or her.

This public duty of the African poet results in the scarcity of poets who write on their private experiences. In the modern Western world, poetry is almost entirely perceived as a medium of private expression. Generally in Africa many private experiences are kept to the persons and not publicized in poems which are bound to be read by others or performed to audiences. While there are African love poems, there is an overwhelming "rhetoric of reticence" (Balogun 22) in that area. In other words, much of the explicitly sexual that appears in Western poetry is selectively excluded by the African poet. Since poetic aesthetics have to do with taste, there seems to be a disavowal of the crudely private in African poetry. Much of the love poetry could praise the beauty of a woman and express the feeling of love, but the poets desist from the naturalistic that characterizes confessional poetry of many American poets of the 1970s.

World-View & Environment

The world-view of a people also affects their aesthetic expectations. Ideas of space and time go into the aesthetic formulation of art in general. Space in traditional Africa relates to land which is very precious. Used or unused, there is hardly any free land. As has been stated in the preceding essay, among the Gikuyu of Kenya, land is so important that who has no small plot is considered poor even if (s)he has plenty of money and cars. In art, the *uli* tradition of the Igbo people which Obiora Udechukwu has done a lot to expose has at its core good use of space. Some places may be crowded with lines but others may be left open. It is a rare ability to relate emptiness to crowd. This may be why the form of the modern African poem, except with poets influenced by Westerners, is rather flexible, relaxed, and relatively loose.

The earth and sky are seen in African folklore as mother and father respectively. Whatever is associated with the earth derives from its fertility. The abundance of images relating to the fauna and flora in African poetry can be traced to views of space, time, earth, and sky. The deeper the roots of the poet in a specific African tradition, the more use of animal and plant imagery. Examples abound in, among others, Clark's *Reed in the Tide* and *Casualties*, p'Bitek's *Song of Lawino*, and Kunene's *The Ancestors and the Sacred Mountain*. In modern African poetry these fauna and flora become sources of symbols, images, figures of speech, and fables. These images are defined by their concreteness rather than the senses they evoke as in much of Western poetry. In poet after poet, these features are indelibly imprinted. In works like *Children of Iroko*, *Labyrinths of the Delta*, *Idanre* and *Eye of the Earth*, space with earth and sky as protagonists gives the concrete setting to the poetry.

Time in traditional Africa follows a natural rhythm of night and day, dry and raining seasons, etc. The time is unhurried, relaxed, and not Swiss-clock precise as in the West. Time is at the disposal of people and not people at the disposal of time. Sayings like "You don't have to hurry to where you will pass the night," and the accusation of impatience when looking at the watch tell a different time from the Western one. Time and space are closely related in cosmic happenings like sunshine, rainfall, night, and day. Many cosmic images which dominate African traditional epics also show up in modern African poetry. In a writer like Soyinka, the cosmic is important in "Idanre" where poet/human being and gods intermingle amidst cosmic happenings.

Formal Considerations

Time can also be associated with the body rhythm which conditions the breath-space in African oral poetry. While there were no lines in traditional African poetry, the breath-space imposed a timing as the performer paused to take a breath. There seems to be some relationship between the breath-space and the line/verse arrangement in modern African poetry. A poet like Kofi Anyidoho appears to consistently obey the breath-space "line" arrangement in his poetry which is meant to be performed. Depending on the model, the lines could be short or long. Usually the short line as in the Yoruba *oriki* and *ijala* and the Zulu *izibongo* is meant to lend weight to individual lines. Osundare's "Earth" is illustrative of this form. On the other hand, in the long line model the performer exhausts maximum time to breathe. Examples of this chant-like style appears in "Love Song" in Ojaide's *Blood of Peace*:

> Hunt of the Antelope takes me unscathed through briars
> Sacrifice to the Princess opens me her bosom
> Love of the Mermaid drives me to the sea of fortune
> Worship of the Goddess transports me to the sky (82).

Okigbo's last poems also reflect this incantatory style of long lines that are really breath-spaces.

The traditional African belief in the cyclical nature of life and things also affects the space and time use in modern African poetry. The belief in the unending shows mainly in traditional songs which can be improvised to go on without a definite end. In modern times, the use of various types of repetition is commonplace. Almost every poet of note in Africa sees repetition as a ready and necessary tool of organization. The repetition could be a mnemonic tool for artistic effect. It could also serve to enhance musicality. The use of repetition of lines which makes the beginning and end of the poem the same is an example of the influence of the belief in the cyclical nature of things. Mazisi Kunene's *The Ancestors and the Sacred Mountain* and Ojaide's *Blood of Peace* have the starting and concluding lines the same in many of their poems.

Parts of the body are copiously alluded to in African oral literature and in modern African writing. This again derives from the sensibility and sensitivity of the people. The field of imagination is close by and immediate, the human body or the known environment. References to fingers, palm/hand, feet, eyes, ears, birthcord, and others are copious. These references touch on the different senses and make the poetry sensuous and concrete. There is little of the abstract in modern African poetry.

Conclusion

Culture and historical experience appear to strongly condition artistic aesthetics, and this applies to modern African poetic aesthetics. In Africa art is functional and this results in the didacticism of the poetry. Didacticism in its own part affects the content of the poetry, whose meaning is meant to be easily decoded by the audience. Didacticism may not openly espouse moral and ethical lessons but may sharpen the consciousness of the anticipated readers/audience. Since the culture demands community/social responsibility, there is a lot of attention paid to socio-cultural, political, and economic issues which affect the poet's people. The poet is like the antenna of his/her people's consciousness.

An oral tradition of performance has impressed modern African poets who exploit the tonal resources of their indigenous languages, borrow the verbal dexterity of the oral tradition, story-telling techniques, and others to compose poems that are dynamic and generate action. The presence of various forms of repetition reinforces the performance aspect of modern African poetry. Lyricism also marks the poetry in its fluidity both internally and externally.

Modern African poetic aesthetics are unique in possessing a repertory of authentic African features. This authenticity manifests itself in the use of concrete images derived from the fauna and flora, proverbs, indigenous rhythms, verbal tropes, and concepts of space and time to establish a poetic form. Besides (and unlike in the West), content is more important than form and images do not aim to reflect the senses. Content is not perceived by poet and audience as extraliterary. The mere fact that foreign languages are used could occasionally create discord in discourse but modern African poetry attempts to reflect indigenous rhythms. In fact, an authentic African world forms the backdrop of modern African poetry.

References and Works Cited

Anyidoho, Kofi. *Earthchild*. Accra: Woeli, 1985.

Asante, Molefi Kete. *The Afrocentric Idea*. Philadelphia: Temple U.P., 1987.

Awoonor, Kofi. *Until the Morning After: Collected Poems 1963. 1985*. Greenfield Center, NY: Greenfield Review Press, 1987.

Balogun, Odun. "The Contemporary Stage in the Development of African Aesthetic," *Okike*, 19 (September 1981).

Bloom, Harold. *The Western Canon: Books and Schools of the Ages*. 1994.

Chimombo, Steve. *Napolo and the Python*. Oxford: Heinemann, 1994.

Chinweizu with Onwuchekwa Jemie and Ihechukwu Madubuike. *Toward the Decolonization of African Literature, Vol. 1.* Enugu: Fourth Dimension, 1980.

Clark, J.P. *A Reed in the Tide.* London: Longman, 1965.

———. *Casualties.* London: Longman, 1971.

Gayle, Addison, ed. *The Black Aesthetic.* New York: Doubleday, 1971.

Irele, Abiola. *The African Experience in Literature and Ideology.* London: Heinemann, 1981.

Kunene, Mazisi. *The Ancestors and the Sacred Mountain.* London: Heinemann, 1982.

Laing, Kojo. *Godhorse.* Oxford: Heinemann, 1989.

Launko, Okimba (Femi Osofisan). *Dream-Seeker on Divining Chain.* Ibadan: Kraft, 1993.

Lo Liyong, Taban. *The Cows of Shambat.* Harare: Zimbabwe Publishing House, 1992.

McMillen, Liz. "Literature's Jeremiah Leaps Into the Fray," *The Chronicle of Higher Education* (September 7, 1994).

Morrison, Toni. *Playing in the Dark: Whiteness and the Literary Imagination.* New York: Vantage, 1993.

Ojaide, Tanure. "Modern African Literature and Cultural Identity," *African Studies Review* 35/3 (December 1992).

———. *Children of Iroko & Other Poems.* Greenfield Center, NY: Greenfield Review Press, 1973.

———. *Labyrinths of the Delta.* NY: Greenfield, 1986.

———. *The Blood of Peace.* Oxford: Heinemann, 1991.

———. "Musical Roots: The Rhythm of Modern African Poetry." *The Middle-Atlantic Writers Association Review,* 7/2 (December 1992).

Okigbo, Christopher. *Labyrinths.* London: Heinemann, 1971.

Osundare, Niyi. *The Eye of the Earth.* Ibadan: Heinemann (Nig.), 1985.

p'Bitek, Okot. *Song of Lawino.* Nairobi: EAPH, 1966.

Soyinka, Wole. *Idanre and Other Poems.* London: Methuen, 1967.

———. *Mandela's Earth.* New York: Random House, 1988.

Stone, Ruth M. *Dried Millet Breaking: Time, Words, and Songs in the Woi Epic of the Kpelle.* Bloomington and Indianapolis: Indiana UP, 1988.

Warren, D.M. & J. Kweku Andrews. "An Ethnoscientific Approach to Akan Arts and Aesthetics." Working Papers in the Traditional Arts. A Publication of the Institute for the Study of Human Issues, Philadelphia (1977).

3

Orality in Recent West African Poetry

L iterary scholars of oral tradition and literature have for long debated the relationship between oral and written literatures. Albert Lord sees the distinction between oral and written kinds of composition as "contradictory and mutually exclusive" (129). Walter J. Ong also distinguishes between written literature and oral tradition. He opines that there is "no satisfactory term or concept to refer to a purely oral heritage" (10–11). Ruth Finnegan, like Ong, accepts the distinction between oral and written traditions but suggests that even the oral is literature. However, she says that the concept of oral literature is unfamiliar (1).

The view of the incompatibility of oral and written compositional styles is supported by the tradition of oral literature which is meant to be read aloud, or at least used as the basis for an oral performance. Curshmann has asked whether it is "really possible to make a strict and methodological valid distinction between written and oral poetry on the basis of composition by motif and pattern, and consequently, by formula (qtd. in Bauml 400). He says that the writer-poet uses the same method of adopting oral characteristics of style for compositional purposes beyond the scope of oral poetry (idem). There is the "deliberate use of formulaic language, composition by motifs and standard patterns" (idem).

Despite this attempt to establish distinctions between oral and written traditions of literature, modern African literature is in a way written oral literature. This description of modern African poetry no doubt arises from the recognition of the double heritage of modern African poets, who have their indigenous African poetic traditions in mind as they write in the Western literary tradition. The orality of written African poetry has been more intensified in recent times by the conscious effort of many West African poets to use the traditional form to reach the generality of the public. The oral in this essay involves folkloric qualities, including the oral character of language and the vocal. There is symmetry in this as oral literature is performed and assumes a vocal quality.

There is a symbiotic relationship between the oral and the written in modern African poetry in which the poetic aim, vision, and practice have fused to produce a poetry that is distinctly oral though written. The oral character of written poetry is generally strong because of the vocal nature of its transmission, being essentially composed to be read aloud. This is more so in West Africa with a strong folkloric tradition which feeds the poets with stylistic models before and during their writing careers. The oral tradition is currently reinforced by the influence of radio and television, which by giving rise to "secondary orality" (Ong 3) is making print to lose some of its influence.

Modern West African poets, especially the younger ones desirous of large audiences, are adapting their poetic techniques to the growing influence of broadcast media and public performance. Thus in recent West African poetry, "the written form is not opposed to the oral form. In fact not only do the two exist side by side... but they often interact" (Tala 9). Ibrahim Tala adds that African "new writers incorporate oral literature in their writing to give flavour of authenticity to their works and to show that as modern Africans they are conscious of a rich source of literary inspiration. They include oral tradition to link their past with their present experience (as a group), to localize the content of their works, to educate fellow Africans and give them confidence in their cultural heritage and to enlighten outsiders and help them get rid of the false impression about African culture acquired from years of cultural misrepresentation"(95–96).

Modern African poets look to traditional African literature for models to express their cultural identity. The oral art is a public one and new West African poets are attempting to relate their form to their articulation of public socio-political concerns. The poets are performing their roles as priests, social reformers, and prophets who speak to their people out of their indigenous tradition to meet the demands of a modern society. Moreover, it is a source of nationalism that a poet projects his/her culture consciously or subconsciously. The strong oral flavor of recent West African poetry has given this poetry not just a distinctive identity but poetic strength. It is in light of the impressive stamp of orality on recent written poetry in West Africa that I intend to discuss the nature, extent, and impact of orality on this poetry. This study will inevitably touch on, among other aspects, the language, techniques, musicality, and form of the poetry.

There is some agreement that "all poetry is in a sense 'oral', since it is written to be read aloud if not publicly performed" (Haynes 138). Besides, poetry in most cultures originated as song. Traditional African poetry is mainly in the form of songs and chants meant to be performed. It is the moment of performance that not only actualizes the oral poem but enlivens it.

West African poets are increasingly writing "oral" poems as a result of their double heritage of Western poetic tradition and their indigenous roots. Though the post-independence generation of Awoonor, Okigbo, Clark, and Soyinka was indebted to the oral tradition, it is with the new generation of poets that orality has become a distinctive mark of West African poetry.

Kofi Awoonor's poems echo his native Ewe rhythms and the poet is highly influenced by his researching Ewe dirges and folktales. "Songs of Sorrow" and "Songs of War" are examples of these oral influences, the former to an actual dirge by an oral artist (Awoonor 85). Wole Soyinka's "Koko Oloro," the poet explains, is a rendition of a children's propitiation song (23). Thus even the poetry of Soyinka, Clark, and early Okigbo who have been vehemently criticized for being imitative of Western modernists (Chinweizu et al. 163–238) is still indebted to the oral tradition of Africa. Awoonor's study of Ewe dirges and folktales already mentioned, like Soyinka's of Yoruba oral drama, and Clark's of Urhobo *udje* songs and the Ijo saga of Ozidi, attests to the familiarity of most of these poets with their native literary traditions.

However, while there is the irony of modern African poets using Western literary techniques to project African culture at independence, there was the lack of strong roots in the oral tradition because of the writers' aims of showing that Africans could write as well as whites and rectifying Western misconceptions and misrepresentations about Africa.

Changing intellectual tastes in audience-conscious new poets who read or perform their poems publicly and a stronger ideological commitment to socio-political and economic change have made recent West African poetry, especially in Nigeria and Ghana, more "oral" than at any time before. In Nigeria there have been regular poetry workshops and public reading sessions in, among other universities, Lagos (Festival of Life), Ibadan, Ife (Okigbo Night), Maiduguri (Poetry Workshop and Writers' Night), Zaria (Creative Writers' Workshop), and Nsukka (Anthill Poetry Series). There have also been big poetry reading occasions in Ghana where the tradition of poetry performance is very strong. There is the poetry recital theater set up in the 1970s which has contributed to the display of orality in modern Ghanaian poetry. It attracts people from all walks of life and it permanently projects poetry as a public event. The program is said to provide "a point of confrontation between poet and audience, and thereby underlining the specifically public concerns of Ghanaian poetry" (Apronti 31).

The major aim of the readings is to reach not only the literati but also the average reader, half-literates and non-literates who understand English, pidgin, and the indigenous languages as the poets articulate their vision for change. With the return to traditional African roots in the use of oral techniques to express socio-political issues in the public readings and performance, the poets compose poems by internally vocalizing words for the specific rhythm they want to articulate.

Significantly, the background of two representatives of the newer poets (Kofi Anyidoho from Ghana and Niyi Osundare from Nigeria) helps to explain the strength of orality in recent West African poetry. Anyidoho took an M.A. in Folklore from Indiana University at Bloomington and a Ph.D. in Comparative Literature from the University of Texas where *Research in African Literatures* which focuses on oral research used to be published. Kofi Awoonor says "Anyidoho's strongest poetic art lies in his capacity to explore the landscape of the dirge, and to discover within the existing tradition which he has learnt so well a clarity of language and depth of sensibility" (Anyidoho 1985: back cover). Similarly, Jawal Apronti has described Anyidoho as one of "the most notable poets" who have absorbed much traditional Ewe poetry (40).

Niyi Osundare who studied English at Ibadan, Leeds (England), and York (Canada) was brought up by his drummer-father in rural Ikere-Ekiti in Nigeria's Ondo State where songs and chants are part of the daily activities of the people. His early upbringing has given him a certain proclivity for drum-accompanied, vocal, and performance-oriented "oral" written poetry. The influences of various Yoruba oral genres such as the *oriki* praise chants and the *ijala* hunters' chants are very strong in his poetry.

Recent modern West African poetry profusely exhibits features of African oral poetic style. This is in contrast to the paucity of such features before now. Composed for performance, traditional African poetry took cognizance of the evanescent nature of drama. Unlike the written poem which can be read and re-read, the audience have only a one-time chance to listen to a song when performed. This makes oral songs generally simple and accessible to the audience. Imbibing this oral quality, the younger West African poets in their radical commitment to change write in an accessible language. While accessibility in poetic communication is relative, there is textual clarity in their poems. This textual clarity can be on the surface level, since the poems may have deeper layers of meaning. Bearing in mind the communicative importance of poetry meant to change society into a better place and picking a cue from the didactic African oral tradition of literature, Osundare writes in *Songs of the Marketplace:*
Poetry is

> the hawker's ditty
> the eloquence of the gong
> the lyric of the marketplace....
> ....

Poetry is
no oracle's kernel
for a sole philosopher's stone

Poetry
is
man
meaning
to
man   (1–2).

Consequently, his "Dawncall" and "Excursion" in *The Eye of the Earth* are examples of poems whose diction, idiom, syntax, and prosody enhance meaning. In "Dawncall" the speaker-poet invites his audience:

Come with me at dawn
When a matchless darkness couples earth and sky
And the world is one starless bed of frigid sweat
Come with me
When trees listen earlessly to the accent
Of the waking wind
Head-deep in the indigo of night   (39).

Similarly, there is clarity of expression in Anyidoho as in "Sound and Silence":

Because because I do not scream
You do not know how bad I hurt

Because because I do not kiss on public squares
You may not know how much I love

Because because I do not swear again and again and again
You wouldn't know how deep I care...   (23).

The vocabulary is familiar but fresh, the syntax and prosody are not distorted to be deliberately poetic. The language flows and is poignant.

This simplicity of communication together with other devices such as repetition helps to impress meaning on the reader's mind. These poets conscious of their responsibility of articulating a positive alternative vision for their societies riddled with socio-political and economic inadequacies in their poetic practice use the modest medium of simplicity. This simplicity should not be seen as poetic weakness but the poets' discretionary and ideological choice to reach more readers and be understood by large audiences at reading sessions.

Simplicity or clarity of expression cannot alone be seen by itself. It is a conglomeration of other stylistic and formal attributes which intermingle to form a folk style. Direct address and dialogue, common features of oral style, are favorite devices of Anyidoho and Osundare, among others. Examples are rife in Anyidoho's *Earthchild* in which "Go Tell Jesus" and "In the High Court of Cosmic Justice" are illustrative of this oral device. In "Go Tell Jesus", the speaker tells the listener:

> Go
> Go tell Jesus
> that his messengers have come
> but have forgotten all his words
> Ask Him if He said
> Men are all equal or
> Men are *un*-equal?   (73).

Similarly, in "In the High Court of Cosmic Justice," the High Priest's invocation is a direct address to deities:

> Adonu Adokli,
> Dancer-Extraordinary
> who threw dust into Master-Drummer's eyes,
> through you I address the Dead Living...
>
> Asase Yaa,
> Sustainer of fertile soil and womb...
> Olokun,
> Supreme Commander of unruly seas...
> Old Shango,
> Controller-General of light and sound and flame...
> Nene Ani,
> Mother-Queen of Earth...
> I invoke you all to our aid...   (76–77).

This same directness of address in traditional African oratory is displayed in many other West African poets. The device of direct address is dramatic and makes the poem very effective in a public reading or performance as the reader-performer will be able to articulate elements of sarcasm, wit, humor, and pun. By enlivening the rendering of the poem, this oral feature in recent West African poetry not only enhances the entertainment quality but also reinforces the communicative effect of the poem.

These poems carry a 'speaking voice,' as Anyidoho, for instance, appears as a revolutionary spokesman in a rally, an occasion for oral address rather than written discourse. The poet's choice of words is thus to make maximum vocal effect. The poet's use of "chronic psychedislocation," "morbid melancholia," and "pre-mortem autopsy" in "Brain

Surgery" is characteristic of oral expression which exploits sound to register sarcasm and humor. This is particularly important in the West African region in which politicians such as S.L. Akintola, K.O. Mbadiwe, and Nnamdi Azikiwe were famous for vocal exploitation of words. Such words as in much of recent West African poetry have their strongest impact on the listener in a recital context rather than on the reader of a work.

The use of dialogue, comments, and exclamation also reinforces the orality of recent West African poetry. Anyidoho's "To Ralph Crowder..." bears these oral qualities:

You may come Crowder
You may come Brother
But Oh Crowder!
   all is not well at home
   all is not well with us
We shall welcome you back home   (112).

"In the High Court of Cosmic Justice" also has these oral dramatic qualities of dialogue, comments, and exclamation which through performance enliven the poetic art.

Atukwei Okai, another Ghanaian poet, also employs dramatic dialogue to underscore the orality of his poetry. His audience-consciousness probably inspired "Prelude" in *Oath of the Fontomfrom*:

You ask:
Which is
My territory
I reply
This is my song.
You ask: By whose authority,
I reply
Who says
I am wrong   (70–71).

In fact, Okai has turned poetry recital into a popular public event in Ghana. His sojourn in Russia which has a strong tradition of poetry recital reinforced his African oral tradition. He is quoted as declaring that "it does not make sense to insist on separating the sound qualities of words from their meaning" (Ogungbesan 49). The titles of his collections reflect the emphasis on performance: *Oath of the Fontomfrom and Other Poems* (1971) and *Lorgorligi Logarithms* (1974). There is an overwhelming use of alliteration to enunciate the vocal tenor of his poetry. There are poems titled "Flower-fall," "pastoral prelude,"

"Fugue for Fireflies," "Dreamdown Communique to Valerieville," "Rhododomdroms in Donkeydom," and "Lorgorligi Logarithms."

Jawa Apronti says of Okai: "The oracular quality of Okai's poetry has been noted by commentators. He combines direct invocation of famous, and comparatively obscure, personages with a playing on the sounds of words that chime in his mind, thus managing to drive home a point many times over" (Ogungbesan 42). The "playing on the sounds of words" typical of Okai is exhibited in:

> My brothers,
>   my people,
>   my brothers:
> Fontomfrom!......Fontomfrom!
> I am
>   the Fontomfrom—
>   listen!
> Of you the living,
> I am
>   the Fontomfrom—
> Fontomfrom.......Fontomfrom!   (20–21).

Though Okai's poetry may be criticized for placing more emphasis on sound at the expense of sense, its orality and entertainment value cannot be disputed. From the examples of Anyidoho, Osundare, and Okai, written poetry in West Africa has been made a live art as in the oral tradition.

Other features of traditional African literature absorbed by modern West African poets are the use of allusion and topicality. *Guardians of the Sacred Word,* a collection of Ewe dirges, and *Sixteen Great Poems of Ifa,* Yoruba divination poems, respectively demonstrate the great use of these two stylistic features in traditional West African poetry. There are allusions and references to persons, gods, places, and events. Sometimes the allusion is plain as in Anyidoho's "Honeycomb for Beechildren" and "Bloomington." In the latter poem, the poet names his colleagues and friends while a student at Bloomington, Indiana. "Hepburn" is an apartment house (37). A more subtle allusion is in "In the High Court of Cosmic Justice" in which the Ghanaian political scene, especially concerning Kwame Nkrumah's achievements and shortcomings, is debated by various characters.

In Osundare's *Eye of the Earth,* there are allusions to "Olosunta," "a huge, imposing rock in Ikere, worshipped yearly during the popular *Olosunta* festival," to "Oroole," a pyramid-shaped rock, also in Ikere, and to "Amoye," Amoye Grammar School. Also in his "Harvestcall," there are allusions to Iyanfoworogi, Oke Eniju, and Ogbese Odo (18–21) and in "Meet me at Okeruku" to Okeruku, "a red-earth district in Ikere" (33). There are many allusions and references to the poet's childhood environment of Ikere in Nigeria's Ondo State as he goes back memory lane to invoke the lost idyll which contrasts with the polluted environment of contemporary times.

In many West African poets' works, there are allusions to socio-political happenings in the poets' respective countries. "Udoji" is illustrative of Osundare's use of topical allusion and he has to append a note to explain the pay hike in Nigeria in 1975 which led to high inflation. Most of these poets seem to be nation-conscious and project a vision of the state as the basis for socio-political change. Since these poems are primarily aimed at nationals of these poets, there will be no problem of obscurity encountered as the persons, places, and events alluded to are public information that an average reader of newspapers, radio listener, and television watcher will be acquainted with. This is directly in the African tradition of songs, especially of abuse and praise, in which allusions made are expected to be understood by the generality of the people.

Rhetoric and oratory in the form of proverbs, praise-names, axioms, and idiomatic expressions are very strong elements of oral literature. Osundare's *Songs of the Marketplace* and *The Eye of the Earth* are replete with traditional rhetoric and oratory. In "Udoji," the poet says:

> when a bribe is too heavy
> it impoverishes the giver   (35).

This is a wise saying as one who bribes with too much is consequently bound to be impoverished. Similarly, in Anyidoho's "Song," there is:

> It is to a tree that a bull is tied
> You do not bypass the palm's branches to tap its wine   (47).

Both *A Harvest of Our Dreams* and *Earthchild* have many proverbial sayings. These proverbial and wise sayings tend to succinctly summarize in a most pungent idiom the context of their appearance.

Praise-name epithets which give a rhetorical flavor to poetry abound in recent West African poetry. For Osundare native to the Yoruba culture, there is a ready tradition of *rara, oriki,* and *ijala* chants to draw from. "Earth," the first poem in *The Eye of the Earth*, is an extended praise-name:

Temporary basement
and lasting roof

first clayey coyness
and last alluvial joy

breadbasket
and compost bed

rocks and rivers
muds and mountains

silence of the twilight sea
echoes of the noonsome tide

milk of mellowing noon
fire of tropical hearth

spouse of the roving sky
virgin of a thousand offsprings
Ogeere amokoyeri   (1).

With myriads of metaphors, the poet weaves names to describe the character and nature of the earth. In the last line of the poem, the earth is "The one that shaves his head with the hoe" (1). "Forest Echoes" is like an *oriki* praise chant to the flora and fauna of the poet's environment. The great forest tree is praised in

Iroko wears the crown of the forest,
town's rafter, roof of the forest
ironwood against the termites of time.

Iroko wears the crown of the forest
its baobab foot rooted against
a thousand storms   (5).

In the same poem, the chameleon is the "aborigine of wood and wind" (8).

Anyidoho's "In the High Court of Cosmic Justice" presents fine examples of the praise-name formula in written poetry. The High Priest invokes the deities thus:

Adonu Adokli
Dancer-Extraordinary
who threw dust into Master-drummer's eyes,
....
Asase Yaa,
Sustainer of fertile soil and womb...

Other deities praised include Olokun, Sango, and Ani. Further on in the same poem, *Dragoligo* is "the strange stranger who displaces his host" (81). The many proverbs and praise-names give a tone of dignity to the poetic voice.

Other features of African oral poetic style absorbed by modern West African poets manifest themselves in the use of grammatical parallelism, noun-pronoun variation, simile, and metaphor. An example of grammatical parallelism is

> Monkey was caught in a trap
> Consider the fate of Rat
> Lizard has lost his tail
> What may become of Fox?
> Chameleon was found out
> Old Frog got drowned last night
> And Cock has lost his voice   (Anyidoho 102).

Parallelism sometimes involves antithetical balance as in "Yesterday was someone's day / Today for someone else" (103). Osundare's "Excursion" and "What the Earth Said" are also illustrative of grammatical parallelism which involves structural repetition and parallelism in syntax and sound. Parallelism gives rise to lexical overlapping as a result of the repetitions of phrases. The latter parts of Anyidoho's "Sound and Silence" and Osundare's "Excursion" and "What the Earth Said" have grammatical variations which give vocative force and imperative tone to the lines.

The use of grammatical parallelism common in oral literature is the expressive way of depicting additive thoughts rather than subordinate ones. It conveys semantic reiteration which in an oral performance registers mnemonic impression. Sometimes, there is the use of "and" to show the cumulative nature of the parallelism; at other times there is none. An example from Osundare's *Eye of the Earth* is:

> of caked riverbeds
> and browned partners
> of baking noons
> and grilling nights
> of earless cornfields
> and tired tubers   (32).

Grammatical parallelism is highly functional in written poetry. It evokes a monotonous rhythmic quality which is aesthetically pleasing when poems are read out.

Pronouns are commonly used in place of nouns at the beginning of sentences in African oral songs. Anyidoho's "Rodney" and "Memory's Call" are pivoted on "we." In another poem,

They call me the Mouther

. . . .

They complain I talk too much without purpose   (79).

Similes and metaphors are common in these poems. In Osundare's *Eye of the Earth*, there are "eyeful glances" (28), "The sky carries a boil of anguish" (27), and "balded plains" (27), among others. Furthermore, as in traditional songs, there are copious examples of nature-oriented, cosmic, and domestic images.

Epithets are copiously used in recent West African poetry as in oral literature. These epithets, indicative of the formulaic nature of oral poetry, are essentials of oral thought processes. This section of Osundare's "Forest Echoes" is an example of the poet's propensity for epithets:

Palm-bound, scalpel-toothed,
the squirrel pierces the tasty iris
of stubborn nuts;
adzeman of the forest,
those who marvel the canine fire
in your mouth,
let them seek refuge in the fluffy grace
of your restless tail   (8).

In many other poems of *The Eye of the Earth*, these epithets occur in alliterative clusters such as "A bevy of birds" and "a barrack of beasts."

The use of the breath-space pause characteristic of African orature is common in Anyidoho. *Earthchild* is significant in modern African poetry as the normal punctuation of written English is ignored for a pause which is graphically reflected by spacing on the printed page. "Sound and Silence," from which I earlier quoted, is an example. This quality gives Anyidoho's poetry a distinctive live quality both visibly on the page and when rendered aloud.

A further quality of recent West African poetry which aligns it to African orature is the musicality. Léopold Sédar Senghor says monotonous rhythm is a distinguishing feature of African poetic compositions. According to him, "*Cette force ordinatrice qui fait le style negre est le rythme*" (Senghor 35). He considers it like inhaling and exhaling air, a rhythm he describes as "*vivant*" and "*libre*." Musical considerations, very oral attributes, inform the poetic features of verbal and structural repetitions and parallelism. Many new West African poets have imbibed the Agisymban stylistic characteristics of the sound of drums, the thud of dancing feet, and melody of tone. The tonal nature of most Black African languages combined with European linguistic rhythms give a peculiar musical quality to recent West African poetry. To reinforce the musicality of the poems, there are repetitions of phrases, lines, and structure. Osundare's "Excursion" and "What the Earth Said" are examples of the musical use to which the poet can put repetitions.

Many poets have experimented with traditional African rhythms. In many cases, the poet superimposes English words over a traditional African musical rhythm. Osundare's poems carry *oriki* and *ijala* rhythms with which Yoruba people are most familiar. In the same vein, Anyidoho taps the Ewe dirge rhythm for his own poetic creations. Sometimes there are poems written to the accompaniment of flutes and drums. This is particularly common with Osundare's poetry, bearing in mind that his father was a master-drummer. Musicality as in Osundare and Anyidoho makes poetry lively and pleasing.

The many examples of oral features so far discussed establish the strong orality of the poetry of Osundare and Anyidoho, two representative new West African poets. This orality is not a poetic fad but a highly functional artistic orientation to realize certain poetic aims, especially to enliven an art which has been torpid in the ivory tower practice to which earlier writers like Okigbo and Soyinka have subjected it. Orality makes poetry very lively, especially with the qualities of direct address, exclamation, and dialogue. These qualities underscore the live and dramatic nature of recent West African poetry. This is directly related to the strong entertainment value of the poetry. In addition to performance which has a physical effect on the audience, it is highly entertaining, more especially with the intellectual delight from proverbs, praise-names, epithets, and allusions. There is also aesthetic fulfillment from the musicality of the poems.

The oral folk style makes the poems highly accessible to a large audience of listeners and readers. The poets use the simple style to convey their vision of society. They articulate clearly the dichotomy between the haves and the have-nots and their desire for an egalitarian and just society. Their major concern is for their message to be understood clearly to have the intended impact of sharpening the consciousness of their readers towards a new and positive socio-political and economic order. The very "oral" form of these poems enhances meaning which seems uppermost in the new poets' minds to fulfill their didactic role.

In conclusion, Osundare and Anyidoho, among other new West African poets, by imbibing oral poetic features have written poems which are better enjoyed when heard than when read silently. With them poetry has been brought down from its former ivory tower status to a popular public art form. These poets appear to have successfully given a new lease of life to poetry which from the many public readings and performances seems now to have regained its traditional popular live form in West Africa, especially in Nigeria and Ghana.

References and Works Cited

Abimbola, Wande, ed. *Sixteen Great Poems of Ifa*. Paris: UNESCO, 1975.

Anyidoho, Kofi. *Elegy for the Revolution*. Greenfield Center, NY: Greenfield Review Press, 1978.

———. *Harvest of Our Dreams*. London: Heinemann, 1984.

———. *Earthchild*. Accra: WOELI, 1985.

———. *Ancestral Logic & Caribbean Blues*. Trenton, NJ: Africa World Press, 1993.

Apronti, Jawa. "Ghanaian Poetry in the 1970s." *New West African Literature*. Ed. Kolawole Ogungbesan. London: Heinemann, 1979.

Awoonor, Kofi, ed. *Guardians of the Sacred Word*. New York: NOK, 1974.

Baumi, Franz H. "The Oral Tradition and Middle High German Literature." *Oral Tradition* 1/2 (1986).

Chinweizu, et al. *Towards the Decolonization of African Literature*. Enugu: Fourth Dimension, 1980.

Finnegan, Ruth. *Oral Literature in Africa*. Nairobi: OUP, 1976.

Haynes, John. *African Poetry and the English Language*. London: Macmillan, 1987.

Lord, Albert. *The Singer of Tales*. Cambridge, MA: Harvard UP, 1960.

Nwoga, Donatus, ed. *West African Verse*. London: Longman, 1976.

Ogungbesan, Kolawole, ed. *New West African Literature*. London: Heinemann, 1979.

Okai, John Atukwei. *Oath of the Fontomfrom and Other Poems*. New York: Simon & Schuster, 1971.

Okpewho, Isidore. *The Epic in Africa*. New York: Columbia UP, 1980.

Ong, Walter J. *Orality and Literacy: The Technologizing of the Word*. London/New York: Methuen, 1982.

Osundare, Niyi. *Songs of the Marketplace*. Ibadan: New Horn, 1983.

———. *The Eye of the Earth*. Ibadan: Heinemann, 1986.

———. *Waiting Laughters*. Lagos: Malthouse, 1991.

Senghor, Léopold Sédar. "Ce que l'homme noir apporte." *Liberte 1: Negritude et Humanisme*. Paris: Seuil, 1964.

Soyinka, Wole. *Idanre & Other Poems*. London: Eyre Methuen, 1967.

Tala, Ibrahim Kashim. *An Introduction to Cameroon Oral Literature*. Yaounde: SOPECAM, 1984.

4

Musical Roots: The Rhythm
of Modern African Poetry

From the beginning poetry and music have been closely related art forms. In fact, the lyric derives from the ancient musical instrument, the lyre. In both African and Western traditions, poetry enhances music, and music enhances poetry in their separate functions. I intend to discuss the manner and function of the musical influence on the rhythm of modern African poetry. I use the term "music" in its very loose sense of meaning the art and science of combining vocal or instrumental sounds or tones in varying melody, harmony, rhythm, and timbre, especially so as to form structurally complete and emotionally expressive compositions. It also means any rhythmic sequence of pleasing sounds. Though "music begins where words are powerless to express" (Pieterse 133), poetry and music are twin arts and necessary companions; hence in African folklore and Western classical tradition, poetry and music tend to be inspired by the same or identical gods or muses. As Amiri Baraka puts it in an interview, "poetry is the sound of music" (Duval 11).

The printed word is not an actualization of the poem except when it is read aloud. This is true of the African and Western traditions that coalesced to form modern African poetry. In Africa it is proverbial that the griot, the singer of tales, "always has a weakness for music, for music is the griot's soul" (Niane 39). It must be borne in mind that in many African languages, poetry and song, which is a musical composition, are synonymous. The African poem, a song or chant, is a combination of words and music to make meaning. However, in a poem language is considered to be more important than music. According to G. Adali-Morty, in his analysis of Ewe poetry, "in traditional folksongs, the words are given prominence over the sound. Though the melody may be charming, it is kept very simple. The sound gives colour and depth to the words. The sound embellishes the ideas, and gives a pleasing background" (Beier 5). It is this complementary function of music and poetry that J.H. Nketia also reinforces when he says:

> Verbal prosodies are combined with musical prosodies, and the emotional depth of the dirge is maintained and strengthened through the combination of language and music (118).

Rhythm is very important in modern African poetry. In reading and performance by the poet or reader, an appropriate rhythm not only creates the *right* atmosphere to facilitate meaning but generates emotional involvement, as well. In both the poet and the reader, there are two basic readings: the internal and the external. The poet internally vocalizes his words to feel the rhythm he wants to create. To achieve this, he uses many musical devices, including varying tonal alternations and figures of sound. With the increasing popularity of secondary orality (Ong 3) and many public performances, rhythm has become one of the major aspects that occupy the forefront of the modern African poet's compositional priorities.

Early modern African poetry was highly influenced by Western poetic traditions. By using English, French, or Portuguese, the modern African poet has partially imbibed the poetic qualities of the language in which he writes. Thus the English iambic pentameter and the French alexandrine seem to be the metric patterns in early Christopher Okigbo and Léopold Sédar Senghor respectively. Lines from *Heavensgate* tend to follow the English iambic rhythmic pattern:

> BEFORE you, mother Idoto
> naked I stand   (Okigbo 3).

Such features in the metropolitan language which give rise to musicality were and are still borrowed by many modern African poets. Rhythmic variations, rhyme, pararhyme, alliteration, assonance, onomatopoeia, and ideophone are thus used for poetic musicality. J.P. Clark's "Night Rain" illustrates this exploitation of musical features innate to the English language:

> What time of night it is
> I do not know
> Except that like some fish
> Doped out of the deep
> I have bobbed up bellywise
> From stream of sleep
> And no cocks crow.
> It is drumming hard here
> And I suppose everywhere
> Droning with insistent ardour upon
> Our roof thatch and shed...
> ....
> So let us roll over on our back
> And again roll to the beat
> Of drumming all over the land

And under its ample soothing hand
Joined to that of the sea
We will settle to our sleep of the innocent and free   (2–3).

Here Clark exploits the sonic resources of the English language, and the
various sound effects result in a rhythm which reflects night rain in the
Nigerian riverine environment. Thus rhythm here is highly evocative,
and the musicality of the poem helps to convey meaning in a sensual,
concrete, and dramatic way.

The Nigerian Christopher Okigbo was highly interested in jazz and
was featured in musicals at school. He admits that musical composers
more than poets have influenced him most in his poetry. According to
him, "when I was working on *Heavensgate* I was working under the
spell of the impressionist composers Debussy, C. Frank Revel..."
(Pieterse 133). Okigbo was also influenced by poets like Baudelaire,
Rimbaud, and Mallarme, to whom "the ultimate goal of poetry should
be the state of music, especially Wagner's music" (Ifere 12). Okigbo
tries to adopt this in "Lament of the Silent Sisters," where the aesthetic
quality of words no longer matters. What matters is how it functions as
a quality of music. Even in *Heavensgate*, Okigbo sacrifices meaning for
musicality as in

For we are listening in cornfields
     among the windplayers,
Listening to the wind leaning over
     its loveliest fragment   (5).

For Okigbo's love of imitating Western poets, Gerald Moore says he

> uses the type of broken melody perfected by T.S. Eliot to evoke the re-
> proachful sadness of abandoned shrines, rotting image, symbols which
> quite naturally carry the whole weight of an African tradition which
> has always concentrated the expression of its values upon them (143).

Okigbo thus sees himself as a music-maker, a composer of sounds.
All through his early poems, the Orpheus personage is regarded as a
bird singing and the image is maintained with different types of birds. In
Heavensgate, the sun-bird image is used: "a sun-bird to mourn a
mother on a spray" (3). This is replaced by that of a weaverbird in
"Limits," where the poet suddenly becomes "talkative like a weaverbird" (23).

There are certain qualities associated with African music and songs.
Awoonor says that the "essential features" of the song "are revealed in
statement, allusion, imagery created through simile or metaphor, and
repetition... repetition of lines or of whole segments. This is both for

emphasis and for creating the emotional poetic lead into other sections of the same poem. They also serve as pauses, and in final position as the rounding up, the poetic finale" (24).

Many ethno-musicologists have published their findings on the characteristic features of African music. These qualities include verbal and structural repetitions, refrains, parallelism, hiatus, monotony, and variation and antithesis. These musical features affect syntax, prosody, diction, and other language aspects of the poem. The choice of liquid sounds in alliterations as in Okigbo's *Heavensgate* is meant to generate a rhythm reflective of water imagery.

The modern African poet, like his counterparts elsewhere, is culturally rooted and carries the sensibility of his people. Consequently, he imbibes the rhythm traditional to his culture. Léopold Senghor says monotonous rhythm is a distinguishing feature of African poetry. He says, *"Cette force ordinatrice qui fait le style nègre est le rythme"* (35). He considers it like inhaling and exhaling air, a rhythm he describes as *"vivant"* and *"libre"* (35). The monotonous rhythm derives from the underlying music in African poetic compositions. The oral breath-space becomes a line in written literature, but the traditional rhythm still persists. Thus musical considerations inform the poetic features of verbal and structural repetitions and parallelism. Copious examples of monotonous rhythm abound in almost every African poet, but especially in poets with a strong African cultural background such as Okot p'Bitek, Mazisi Kunene, J.P. Clark, and later Okigbo. Kunene's "Their Love" is one of many examples:

> Such was the joy of their love;
> Like sunrays cutting through the evening forest
> Like a cluster of white cranes circling the horizon
> Like twins whispering to each other
> Like a gigantic mountain thrust against the sky
> Like happy crowds assembled for the festival
> Like a beautiful vessel headed by young girls
> Like a gift of friendship before a long journey
> Like mists, dangling low over the earth   (28).

Here the repetitions form a cluster of similes to reinforce a point. Apart from indicating emphasis, the repetition and its accompanying monotonous rhythm could be most important in a ritual poem such as Birago Diop's "Viaticum" in creating a solemn atmosphere.

Negritude writers like Aimé Césaire, Léopold Senghor, and Léon Damas imbibed the Agisymban rhythms. The following lines from Senghor's "Congo" are illustrative of this ancient African rhythm:

Oho! Congo oho! Pour rythmer ton nom grand sur les eaux
sur les fleuves sur toute memoire
Que j'emeuve le voix des koras, Koyate! L'encre
du scribe est sans memoire.
Oho! Congo couchees dans ton lit de forêt, reine
sur l'Afrique domptee
Que les phallus des monts portent haut ton pavillon
(Anthologie 168)

The rhythm is full of the energy and liveliness that Senghor says characterize African poetry. The tonal nature of Black African languages combined with European rhythms, give a distinctive mark to African poetry.

Many modern African poets have experimented with traditional African rhythms. In many cases, the poet superimposes European words on a traditional African rhythm. Occasionally, a poem's rhythm is lifted or distorted from an existing traditional musical composition. For example, a section of "Labyrinths of the Delta" strongly echoes a song in an Urhobo folktale. The original folksong reads thus when transliterated and translated:

Uro bio ogbeyin rhe
tue tue
Uro bio ogbeyin rhe
tue tue
Ogbeyin ru vwe
Oru vwe abo vwirhi
tue tue
Ogbeyin ru vwe
Oru vwe awo vwirhi
tue tue
Uro bio ogbeyin rhe
tue tue-e

(Current, bring back the tortoise
gently, gently
The tortoise tortured me
he broke my hands
gently, gently
The tortoise tortured me
he broke my legs
gently, gently
Current, bring back the tortoise
gently, gently)

The relevant part of "Labyrinths of the Delta" reads thus:

> Turn the tortoise back, O waters,
> Bring him back
> Spare him mishap on the way
> Bring him back to me;
> He broke not only my hands
> But also my legs and ribs;
> Bring him back to me
> Spare him mishap on the way here
> And let the villain taste
> What he inflicted on me
> From my own hands   (Ojaide 26).

This shows not only the conscious and sometimes subconscious use of traditional rhythms by many African poets but also the rootedness of the individual poet in the traditional rhythms of his people.

The practice of using traditional musical rhythms is common with poets such as Kunene, Awoonor, Okot p'Bitek, Soyinka, Anyidoho, and Osundare, who look to the African folkloric tradition in their poetic creations. Other poets, including Senghor and Okigbo, write poems to the accompaniment of traditional musical instruments. The poet matches his choice of accompaniment with rhythms tradition-ally associated with such poems. This makes the poetry lively and contributes a pleasing aspect to the art. Above all, it helps to create the necessary atmosphere for the poet to communicate his ideas and feelings.

There are certain poetic forms with innate generic rhythms. Thus Africans writing dirges, abuse songs, praise chants, odes, and other po-etic forms instinctively fall back on traditional African rhythms associ-ated with the forms they want to use. Consequently, Kofi Awoonor's "Songs of Sorrow," which is indebted to the Ewe dirge tradition, carries the slow mournful music for which the Ewe dirge is famous. Awoonor's research into Ewe dirges, which resulted in the publication of *Guardians of the Sacred Word*, like Soyinka's research into Yoruba folk drama, should have opened to him a storehouse of folkloric wealth. The first two stanzas of "Songs of Sorrow" register the slow mournful rhythm of the dirge:

> Dzogbese Lisa has treated me thus
> It has led me among the sharps of the forest
> Returning is not possible
> And going forward is a great difficulty
> The affairs of this world are like chameleon faeces
> Into which I have stepped
> When I clean it cannot go.

I am on the world's extreme corner,
I am not sitting in the row with the eminent
But those who are lucky
Sit in the middle and forget
I am on the world's extreme corner
I can only go beyond and forget   (Moore and Beier 98).

The Yoruba-speaking poets writing in English have absorbed the *ijala* and *oriki* chant rhythms of their people. *Ijala* and *oriki* are praise chants, the former exclusive to hunters and the latter associated with the chiefly class. In *Ogun Abibiman*, Soyinka exhorts:

In time of race, no beauty slights the duiker's
In time of hunt, the lion's grace is holy
In time of flight, the egret mocks the envious
In time of strife, none vies with Him
Of seven paths, Ogun, who to right a wrong
Emptied reservoirs of blood in heaven
Yet raged with thirst...   (7).

Similarly, Niyi Osundare in *The Eye of the Earth* sings the Earth's *oriki*:

Temporary basement
and lasting roof

first clayey coyness
and last alluvial joy

breadbasket
and compost bed

rocks and rivers
muds and mountains

silence of the twilight sea
echoes of the noonsome tide

milk of mellowing moon
fire of tropical hearth

spouse of the roving sky
virgin of a thousand offsprings

Ogeere amokoyeri   (1).

The use of incantatory rhythm is particularly effective in *The Eye of the Earth*, as Osundare dexterously balances one line against another. He also uses *oriki* rhythms in *Moonsong* as Soyinka does in *Mandela's Earth*, especially in "Muhammad Ali at the Ringside, 1985."

Though not of Yoruba origin, Christopher Okigbo uses the *ijala* incantatory rhythm in "Lament of the Masks," a poem in praise of the great Anglo-Irish poet W.B. Yeats. The poem's second and third sections are most exhilarating in rhythmic vibrancy:

II   WAGGONER of the great Dawn—
       For it is forbidden to mention your name—

       How many beacon flames
       Can ever challenge the sun?

       Water of baptism,
       Ladder to the ethereal ivory tower—

       Ten thousand rivers
       Can never challenge the sea.

       Thunder above the earth,
       Sacrifices too huge for vulture—

       Twenty thousand cannons
       Must still do homage to your breath.

       Hunter of elephants,
       Earth tremor upon the land—

       For the time has come O Poet,
       To descant your praise-names—

III   THEY THOUGHT you would stop pursuing
           the white elephant
       They thought you would stop pursuing
           the white elephant
       But you pursued the white elephant without
           turning back—
       You who charmed the white elephant with
           your magic flute
       You who trapped the white elephant like a
           common rabbit
       You who sent the white elephant tumbling
           into your net—
       And stripped him of his horns, and made them
           your own—
       You who fashioned his horns into ivory
           trumpets—
       They put you into the eaves thatch
       You split the thatch

They poured you into an iron mould
You burst the mould...   (Maxwell and Bushrui xiii–xiv).

This form of repetition, unique to the hunter's chant, gives a distinctive African flavor to the rhythm of modern African poetry.

Other African poets have experimented with indigenous rhythmic patterns associated with particular poetic forms. Abuse and praise song patterns are many. By using these poetic forms, African poets attempt to match rhythm with themes so as to create the necessary atmosphere for the communication of their ideas and feelings. Also these rhythms, as in Okigbo's "Lament of the Masks," give a pleasing quality and African identity to the poems.

In traditional Africa the song is generally synonymous with poetry. As Awoonor puts it, "The song in the Ewe tradition is structurally the poem" (24). Two poets whose poetry started in African languages as songs before being translated by themselves into English are Okot p'Bitek in *Song of Lawino* and Mazisi Kunene in *The Ancestors and the Sacred Mountain*. Okot p'Bitek is said to have started in 1954 to write in Acoli the long poem that turned out in English to be *Song of Lawino* twelve years later. Since the song is meant to be performed, *Song of Lawino* has the attributes of the traditional African song, which is highly musical. The rhythm of the poem is very lively and charged, and there is the impression that, though the poem is in English, it carries its original Acoli musical rhythms. On the printed page, the accompaniments are not there or mentioned, but there is an apparent suggestion of the clapping of hands, drumming, and dancing, which generally accompany African songs. Lawino, who defends traditional African culture being abandoned by her Acoli husband and her rival Clementine, proudly asserts:

When the daughter of the Bull
Enters the arena
She does not stand there
Like stale beer that does not sell,
She jumps here
She jumps there.
When you touch her
She says "Don't touch me!"   (34).

In *Song of Lawino*, Okot p'Bitek uses traditional African rhythms to convey the celebration of African culture. The ecstatic rhythm imbues the poetic viewpoint with romantic qualities and suggests the poet's personal nostalgic approval of Lawino's position as a defender of African culture and an opponent of indiscriminate copying of Western culture by Africans.

Mazisi Kunene is a Pan-Africanist who strongly preaches the adoption of indigenous languages as a means of literary communication in Africa. He wonders why

> writers who do not write in African languages and traditions have come to represent African writing! It is as though a Conrad were to be said to be writing Polish literature even when he was writing in English only because his country of origin was Poland (xix).

Thus originally written in Zulu, the poems of *The Ancestors* carry the rhythm that is innate to the Zulu language. Undoubtedly, the use of repetition is the most unique quality of these poems. "Their Love" and "The Unhappy Composer" have already been noted for the repetitive quality of Kunene's poetry. Also in "Ecstasy of a Song," there is ecstatic music:

> I am the burning forest
> Whose great flames do not cease
> Despite the age of the earth.
> I wear the blue garments of the sky
> I ride a cyclone
> I wander freely in the path of light
> I pluck the luxuriant plants of dreams
> I build a mountain opposite the space of Nohhoyi.
> I say: "Fill the rivers
> Fill them with rain
> Torment the fools with singing
> Sing to the world!"   (7)

Here there is the ecstatic rhythm of Zulu praise chants as in the *izibongo*.

Kunene uses traditional rhythms to affirm faith in the African poetic heritage. This corresponds with his desire for contemporary Africans to imbibe the virtues of the ancestors whose heroism, courage, and ethical qualities, the poet believes, will help solve many modern problems, including apartheid. His *Zulu Poems* and *Ancestors and the Sacred Mountain* appear able to project an atmosphere with rhythms, and this helps the poet to communicate meaning effectively.

From the discussion it is clear that music in its various rhythmic patterns is a potent force in African poetry. Its omnipresence is functional. Since poetry comes out mainly when vocalized, music gives it a pleasing quality. The polyrhythms give monotony and variation. The rhythms give an emotional impact to the poems, an impact as important as others. In addition, the appropriate rhythms which music generates in the poems create a particular atmosphere which again helps to realize themes. The place of music may be stronger in ritual or religious poems as in early Okigbo, but it remains a necessary component of African poetry.

In conclusion, various musical patterns, some alien and others traditional African, have placed their mark on modern African poetry. This music has gone as far as affecting not only the rhythm of the poetry but the diction, prosody, syntax, and form, as well. In fact, music, or rhythm, where appropriate, has raised the level of poetry, as in Okigbo's *Poems Prophesying War* and Soyinka's *Ogun Abibiman* to a heroic and sublime pitch. Above all, music helps to give modern African poetry a distinctive identity.

References and Works Cited

Awoonor, Kofi, ed. *Guardians of the Sacred Word.* New York: NOK, 1974.

Beier, Ulli. *Introduction to African Literature.* London: Longman, 1984.

Clark, J.P. *A Reed in the Tide.* London: Longman, 1965.

Duval, Elaine I. "Reasserting and Raising Our History: Interview with Amiri Baraka." *Obsidian* II/3 (Spring 1988): 1–17.

Ifere, Funmilayo. "Musicality in Christopher Okigbo's Poetry." Long essay, University of Maiduguri, 1985.

Kunene, Mazisi. *The Ancestors and the Sacred Mountain.* London: Heinemann, 1982.

Maxwell, D.F.S., and S.B. Bushrui. *W.B. Yeats: 1865–1965 Centenary Essays.* Ibadan: Ibadan UP, 1965.

Moore, Gerald. *The Chosen Tongue: English Writing in the Tropical World.* London: Longman, 1969.

Moore, Gerald, and Ulli Beier. *Modern Poetry from Africa.* Harmondsworth: Penguin, 1967.

Niane, D.T., ed. *Sundiata.* Harlow: Longman, 1979.

Nketia, J.H. *Funeral Dirges of the Akan People.* Achimota: Longman, 1955.

Ojaide, Tanure. *Labyrinths of the Delta.* Greenfield Center, NY: Greenfield Review Press, 1986.

———. Review of *The Ancestors and the Sacred Mountain* by Mazisi Kunene. *Liwuram: Journal of the Humanities* 1 (1985): 77–80.

Okigbo, Christopher. *Labyrinths.* London: Heinemann, 1971.

Ong, Walter J. *Orality and Literacy: The Technologizing of the Word.* New York: Methuen, 1982.

Osundare, Niyi. *The Eye of the Earth.* Ibadan: Heinemann Nigeria Ltd, 1986.

p'Bitek, Okot. *Song of Lawino.* Nairobi: East Africa Publ. House, 1966.

Pieterse, Cosmo, ed. *African Writers Talking.* London: Heinemann, 1972.

Senghor, Léopold Sédar. "*Ce que l'homme noir apporte.*" *Liberte I: Negritude et humanisme.* Paris: Seuil, 1964.

————. *Anthologie de la nouvelle poésie nègre et malgache de langue francaise.* Paris: Presse Universitaires de France, 1972.

Soyinka, Wole. *Ogun Abibiman.* London: Rex Collings, 1976.

5

The Changing Voice of History: Contemporary African Poetry

The term "contemporary" generally applies to something of or in the style of the present or recent times. Because of its short history, written African poetry, excluding that of the pioneering period, could be taken as contemporary. Contemporary African poetry is poetry written by Africans in our time; that is, works published between about 1960 and now (1988). It is poetry which is not more than thirty years old and thus literally belongs to the same generation.

Contemporary African poetry presents two trends which can be described as old and new and are particularly divergent in thematic and technical preoccupations. There is a gradual parting of ways between those poets directly influenced by Western, especially English, modernist poets and the younger poets who are highly influenced by traditional African poetic techniques and are preoccupied with socio-economic matters and contemporary political issues. The younger poets are unlike their culture-obsessed and apolitical seniors. They attempt to 'decolonise' African poetry by shedding Western poetic conventions such as rhyme, regular stanzas, and figures of sound.

The focus of this essay will be on the divergence between the older and younger poets of contemporary Africa. As a result of this approach, the essay will be more of a comparative study of the two groups in the generation. In addition, there will be some emphasis on Nigerian poets, since Nigerian national and literary experiences are fairly representative of Africa. There will be statements in this essay which may appear as generalizations because of my attempt to limit illustrations.

Most of the younger African poets have had the advantage of reading and studying the older poets, whose weaknesses they try to avoid. Highly educated, mainly abroad, most of the young writers have Ph.D.s: Kofi Anyidoho, Niyi Osundare, Jack Mapanje, Catherine Acholonu, and Funso Aiyejina, among others. These are unlike the group of Wole Soyinka, Christopher Okigbo, J.P. Clark, Kofi Awoonor, Lenrie Peters, and Okot p'Bitek with mainly first degrees. The educational background of the writers is important because it seems the old were out to prove their talent; that is, they wanted to impress. Hence, they seem to be self-conscious in their writings. In any case, the younger ones appear to have a love-hate relationship with the older group. They admire the innate talent of their literary elders and are inspired by them, but reject their preoccupations and techniques. The older ones seem to them conservative in poetic ideas and practice and too formal in their imitative techniques.

Historical circumstances affecting society, culture, politics, and the economy are mainly responsible for the differences between the old and the new in poetic choices. The 'new poetry' is a development from and yet a deliberate reaction against the old. Echoes of Okigbo's style, especially of his musicality, are heard in Harry Garuba's *Shadow and Dream and Other Poems*, Funso Aiyejina's *Letter to Lynda and Other Poems*, Kofi Anyidoho's *Elegy for the Revolution*, and Tanure Ojaide's *Children of Iroko and Other Poems*. Also Jared Angira's *Cascades* is laced with Okigbo's word-play and rhythmic movement. Similarly, echoes of Soyinka are rife in Odia Ofeimun's *The Poet Lied* and Kobena Eyi Acquah's *The Man Who Died*. While a few of the old (Okigbo and Okot p'Bitek) are dead, most of them are still living and writing. Soyinka's *Ogun Abibiman* appeared in 1976, Kofi Awoonor's *The House by the Sea* in 1978, Kwesi Brew's *African Panorama* in 1981, Lenrie Peters's *Selected Poetry* with "new poems" in 1981 and J.P. Clark's *State of the Union* in 1985. Thus the two groups overlap. There may be a difference between those poets born in the early 1930s and those of the late 1940s or later in the historical and cultural experiences which determined their poetic inspirations, but they all belong to our time.

Dates are not very reliable in establishing a distinction between the old and the new poets, but a dichotomy can be drawn between poetry written from about 1960 to the mid-1970s and from then to the present. As the older poets of the age have changed in their preoccupations and techniques, some of the qualities of the younger poets abound in the old. For instance, J.P. Clark turns from culture and his geographical environment to poetry which has bearing on contemporary issues in *State of the Union*. In this slim collection, Clark deals with social matters such as the menace of robbers, the gap between the rich and the poor, the effect of oil exploration, and the anxiety which makes Nigerians join new churches. Conversely, some qualities of the old abound in the new as in Jack Mapanje's interest in culture in *Of Chameleon and Gods* (1981). Mapanje uses Malawian myths and legends to express the contemporary state of things around him. However, the intensity of some qualities isolates the younger poets into a unique group.

A major thematic preoccupation of the poets of the early 1960s is culture . Okigbo, Clark, Soyinka, Awoonor, and p'Bitek, among others, dealt with African culture from their individual perspectives. Clark and

Soyinka both treat *abiku*, the wanderer-child. Soyinka's "Dedication," "Koko Oloro," and "Idanre" are culturally rooted in the Yoruba world. Okigbo expresses the validity of Igbo cultural values before the assailing Western Christian values in *Heavensgate*. Kofi Awoonor in "I Heard a Bird Cry" (*Night of My Blood*, 1971) asks the dead to guard and guide the living lest they fall into shame. The same theme is echoed in "Songs of Sorrow." *Rediscovery* and *Night of My Blood* expose the Ewe culture. The cultural concern of these poets at that time is understandable. Most African countries became politically independent between 1957 and 1963. The spirit of nationalism and patriotism was riding high waves as "the wind of change" blew across the continent. There was hope and optimism as Africans felt their condition would improve, since their destiny would be in their own hands. Colonialism had been economically exploitative and politically and socially enslaving. Colonialism was justified by Europeans on the grounds that Africans had no culture. At independence Africans wanted to show to the outside world that they had a vibrant culture, which was not inferior to the colonial master's Western one. This gave rise to the portrayal of African culture.

The cultural concern in African poetry took the form of a conflict between the indigenous and the alien. Gabriel Okara expresses the conflict of cultures in symbolic terms in "Piano and Drums:"

> When at break of day at a riverside
> I hear jungle drums telegraphing
> the mystic rhythm, urgent, raw
> like bleeding flesh, speaking of
> primal youth and the beginning,
> I see the panther ready to pounce,
> the leopard snarling about to leap
> and the hunters crouch with spears poised.
> And my blood ripples, turns torrent,
> topples the years and at once I'm
> in my mother's lap a suckling;
> at once I'm walking simple
> paths with no innovations,
> rugged, fashioned with the naked
> warmth of hurrying feet and groping hearts
> in green leaves and wild flowers pulsing.
> Then I hear a wailing piano
> solo speaking of complex ways
> in tear-furrowed concerto:
> of far-away lands

and new horizons with
coaxing diminuendo, counterpoint,
crescendo. But lost in the labyrinth
of its complexities, it ends in the middle
of a phrase at a daggerpoint.
And I lost in the morning mist
of an age at a riverside keep
wandering in the mystic rhythm
of jungle drums and the concerto   (Okara 20).

The drums represent African culture, while the piano represents the
Western. The poet does not take a position in the conflict and allows
himself to be overwhelmed by the two cultures.

Kofi Awoonor also expresses cultural conflict in "The Weaver Bird,"
where the bird symbolises the West and its cultural values. He says:

The weaver bird built in our house
And laid its eggs on our only tree
We did not want to send it away
We watched the building of the nest
And supervised the egg-laying.
And the weaver returned in the guise of the owner
Preaching salvation to us that owned the house.
They say it came from the west
Where the storms at sea had felled the gulls
And the fishers dried their nets by lantern light
Its sermon is the divination of ourselves
And our new horizons limit at its nest
But we cannot join the prayers and answers of the communicants.
We look for new homes every day,
For new altars we strive to rebuild
The old shrines defiled from the weaver's excrement
                                        (Awoonor-Williams 16).

Africans allowed the alien Western values to influence them and with
time these values became most difficult to resist. Also Okigbo and
p'Bitek in their different ways convey this cultural conflict in *Heavensgate* and *Song of Lawino* respectively. The themes of African culture
and of culture conflict became spent after the middle of the 1960s. This
is probably because Africa's political problems became so overwhelming that culture was relegated to the background in the face of more immediate problems of political inefficiency and corruption.

The major trend in African poetry after the early 1960s, a period
which coincides with the first experience of self-rule, is political satire.

The experience of Africans ruling themselves was unpleasant and disappointing. Political independence was rife with various forms of corruption, which did not allow for the anticipated economic growth at the expiration of colonialism. Coups and civil wars gripped many countries. In Nigeria where a civil war raged after two military coups, Okigbo, Soyinka, Clark, and Chinua Achebe wrote poems inspired by the socio-political events. Kofi Awoonor's *The House by the Sea* was inspired by the political factionalization in Ghana, which led to his arrest and detention by the military authorities. Okot p'Bitek's *Song of Lawino* and *Song of Prisoner* express the political differences, tribalism, tyranny and victimisation in Uganda.

Lenrie Peters satirizes African leaders who lord it over their subjects. In *Satellites* this phenomenon is dramatized caustically in "In the Beginning":

> 'I see
> But my children—
> beg pardon Sir,
> will they go to school?'
> Later!
> 'Will they have food to eat
> and clothes to wear?'
> Later I tell you!
> 'Beg pardon Sir;
> a house like yours?'
> Put this man in jail   (84).

The leader is angry at being shown the wide gap between him and his subjects. He put himself in an exclusive privileged class and cares not for the sorry plight of his subjects. There is thus awareness of political happenings in Africa by the older poets. Lenrie Peters may not be as ideologically conscious as many of the younger writers, but his concern for the people in "In the Beginning" sounds genuine.

There came a shift from the cultural and the political to socio-economic matters as economic hardships began to tell excruciatingly on the African populace. The influence of the times is in this regard responsible for the younger writers' preoccupation with socio-economic problems of their environment. After all, the poet is the sensitive part of his society and he articulates its joys and sorrows. Niyi Osundare in "Udoji" says:

> We ask for food and water
> to keep our toiling frames
> on the hoe
> but they inundate us with Udoji   (35).

Chief Jerome Udoji headed a Salary Review Panel that awarded pay increases, which galloped the inflation rate in Nigeria in 1975. This immediately brings to mind Okigbo's reference to the Haragin Commission which also raised salaries in 1945. In any case, the socio-economic orientation indicates the new writers' commitment to social, ideological, and class consciousness. While most of the new poets are proletarian in tendencies, some such as Jared Angira, Niyi Osundare, and Ada Ugah are avowed Marxists.

There is a marked concern for the condition of the people, the masses, as never before. To Angira,

> Public holidays
> Are the only fringe benefits
> Of the poor   (87).

In "Obbligato from the public gallery," he expresses the public mistrust of and disaffection with political abstractions and diversionary measures of the government. He says:

> The public now wants bread
> At least to breed tomorrow.
>
> The public now wants rice
> At least to rise tomorrow.
>
> The public is tired
> Of following the rainbow   (88).

Osundare's "Excursions" in *Songs of the Marketplace* exposes the awful plight of the common people who are neglected by the rulers:

> several government people
> have passed through these streets
> several Mercedes tyres have drenched
> gaunt road lines in sewer water
> several sanitary inspectors have come
> in formidable helmets and gas masks
> but rot and *tanwiji* escape
> the uniformed eye
> poverty is an invisible thing   (9).

"Sule Chase" in which a common man who steals a three-kobo bread to survive is pursued and lynched by the cheats of society reiterates the poet's concern for the masses. Ada Ugah's *Songs for the Talakawa* is highly Marxist. And Syl Cheney-Coker's "Peasants" reinforces the strong concern of the new writers for the common people:

the agony of imagining their squalor but never knowing it
the agony of cramping them in roach infected shacks
the agony of treating them like chattel slaves
the agony of feeding them abstract theories they do not understand
the agony of their lugubrious eyes and bartered souls
the agony of giving them party cards but never party support...(27).

The ideological and proletarian commitment of the younger poets has its consequence on the type of poetry they write. The poetry sounds propagandistic in the sense of being very rhetorical, passionate, and audience-conscious. It is poetry which is meant to be declaimed, especially when read out to large audiences as now obtains in Ghana. Kofi Anyidoho and Kobena Eyi Acquah read their poems to very large audiences in Ghana as is traditionally done in the Soviet Union. The rhetoric of "Peasants" is illustrative of the new poetry, which aims at generating bad feelings towards the haves and sympathy towards the have-nots.

Content and meaning are very important in distinguishing the new poetry from the old. Christopher Okigbo at the Kampala Conference of African Writers in 1965 is said to have told his fellow writers that he did not read his poetry to non-poets. He also told an interviewer at the BBC Transcript Centre that he did not set out in his poetry with any meaning in mind. On many occasions Okigbo made music at the expense of meaning. Wole Soyinka wrote such difficult poetry as if for a côterie. Poems such as "Dawn" and "The Dreamer" in *Idanre and Other Poems* illustrate his obscurity and difficulty. In much of Soyinka's pre-October 1966 poems of *Idanre*, he sacrifices meaning for alliterative jingles. "The Dreamer" again is an example:

Higher than trees a cryptic crown
Lord of the rebel three
Thorns lay on a sleep of down
And myrrh; a mesh
Of nails, of flesh
And words that flowered free
A cleft between the birches
Next year is reaping time
The fruit will fall to searchers
Cleansed of mould
Chronicles of gold
Mourn a fruit in prime.
The burden bowed the boughs to earth
A girdle for the see
And bitter pods gave voices birth

A ring of stones
And throes and thrones
And incense on the sea   (17).

It is apparent that the poet does not aim at clarity, hence the complex syntax, fragmented impressions, and emphasis on sound.

The difficulty and obscurity of Soyinka, Okigbo, and others of their group are resultant from their literary influences. Lewis Nkosi observes that "among the Nigerian poets the initial enthusiasm for Hopkins, Yeats, Eliot and Pound seems...vastly excessive" (127). He goes further to say that "among Okigbo's generation, a generation weaned on Eliot, Pound and the Classics, a certain notion rapidly gained ground that to be taken seriously at all poetry not only had to be made 'new' in the Poundian sense but that it had to be made difficult as well" (155). These poets were influenced by Western modernist poets whose techniques of fragmentation, allusiveness, difficulty, and obscurity they imbibed. There was the attempt by these African poets to be poetic in the Western sense by being archaic in the use of diction and syntax. Apart from sounding like some of the foreign writers (Clark like Hopkins, Okigbo like Pound, and Soyinka like Eliot), they employed a mythopoetic and masonic diction, which is not accessible to most readers (Gibbs 200–212). Theirs has been harshly described as "stiff, pale, academic poetry, slavishly imitative" (Chinweizu 3).

This contrasts with the new poets who are influenced by traditional African poetic techniques. It is ironical that the group of African poets who focused on African culture and value systems did so with alien poetic techniques. However, the new poets who focus on the ordinary people of society use traditional African folk literary techniques. There is a relationship between the private nature of some of the themes of the older group and the difficult language used in expressing them. The new African writer who is public in his treatment of themes, conscious of an audience, is unpretentious, clear and simple in expression. In fact, he is 'unpoetic' in the old way because he employs the syntax of prose. Because it has a speaking voice, the poetry flows, unlike the occasionally stilted poetry of Clark and Soyinka. The new writer models his work on traditional African poetry, whose syntax is not much different from that of prose and in which what makes poetry is the intensity of verbal expression and not archaisms and other 'poetic' mannerisms. Thus the new poet sets out to make meaning. There is a new directness and clarity of expression in the simple images and proverbs used. Osundare's "Poetry is" in *Songs of the Marketplace* is a kind of poetic manifesto of the emergent group:

Poetry is
not the esoteric whisper
of an excluding tongue
not a claptrap
for a wondering audience
not a learned quiz
entombed in Grecoroman lore

Poetry is
a lifespring
which gathers timbre
the more throats it plucks
harbinger of action
the more minds it stirs

Poetry is
the hawker's ditty
the eloquence of the gong
the lyric of the marketplace
the luminous ray
on the grass's morning dew

Poetry is
what the soft wind
musics to the dancing leaf
what the sole tells the dusty path
what the bee hums to the alluring nectar
what rainfall croons to the lowering eaves

Poetry is
no oracle's kernel
for a sole philosopher's stone
Poetry
is
man
meaning
to man   (3).

This poem is an indictment of the difficulty and obscurity associated
with the poetry of Soyinka and Okigbo. Titles such as Osundare's
Songs of the Marketplace, Village Voices and Ugah's *Songs of Talakawa*
indicate an attempt by the new poets to match the concern for the ordinary people with clarity of expression. The poetic aims of the old and

the new poets thus make language a major difference between the two strands of contemporary African poetry.

The older poets are more musical than the newer ones. In *Heavensgate* Okigbo gets relief in withdrawing from unpleasant church atmosphere, saying:

> For we are listening in cornfields among windplayers,
> listening to the wind leaning over its loveliest fragment   (5).

Here the poet is carried away by the liquid and alliterative sounds of *l*. Okigbo's musicality generally obscures meaning. Soyinka's alliterations, as in "The Dreamer," "To My First White Hairs," and "Malediction," are great impediments to comprehension. The new writers as in the traditional African context find meaning more important than music, which is supposed to be a non-distracting accompaniment. Repetitions of words, word-groups, and lines in the Okigbo fashion are mainly to make music or to sound sophisticated. J.P. Clark experiments on sprung rhythm in poems modelled on Hopkins. "Ibadan Dawn" written after "Pied Beauty" is an example of Clark's use of foreign rhythmic patterns:

> Mist-hung curtains, adrizzle-damp, draw, fall
> Apart, spring a forward catch in the sky
> That swift over us spreads, all
> Of a lift, this fresh burst of blue, freckled dye
> In running decks
> Of quicksilver flakes and flecks.... (*A Decade of Tongues*, 16).

However, in the new writing repetitions are more for emphasis and mnemonic effects than for musicality. The musicality is incidental.

It is sometimes argued that what the new generation gains in content and meaning is at the expense of "literary merit" and craftsmanship of their older colleagues. Ken Goodwin, for example, sees a "detached non-political stance" (qtd. in Bamikunle 91) in the culture-suffused poetry of the Soyinka-Okigbo generation. This "non-political stance," which probably means a non-ideological position, seems to be seen as responsible for the craftsmanship in Okigbo, Clark, Soyinka, Peters, and Awoonor, among others. Ken Goodwin also notices the movement "towards political radicalism and indigenisation," which has led to simplification of the English style of the new writers (idem). This difference can also be seen in the older generation's acceptance of Western conventional view of literature, including art for art's sake, and the new writers' upholding a rather traditional African concept of literature as utilitarian. This functional view of literature has come to be associated with socio-economic liberation of the common people and the exploited.

The radicalism of the new poetry is set in nation-states, unlike the culture and nature-centered poetry before it. Even an old poet like Clark writing the new poetry sets his poetic ideas in Nigeria in *State of the Union*. The new writers whether in Ghana, Nigeria, South Africa, Uganda, or Kenya are nation-oriented. There is the desire to transform the nation from a backward state into a shining example of a modern African country. There are many allusions to socio-historical national experiences. Kofi Anyidoho's *Elegy for the Revolution* and Angira's *Cascades* are representative of this trend. Angira might be living in Tanzania when much of *Cascades* was written, but the poems are mainly directed at Kenya.

On one level, therefore, the new poetry is more 'local' than that before it. This has something to do with changing intellectual and literary tastes in Africa. Most of the Western modernist-influenced African poets tended to cherish the "universal." These poets wrote such poems as "Cry at Birth," "Night Rain," "Season," "Dawn," and "I Think It Rains," which could be said to be universally applicable because of their nature-orientation. There seems to be "a determined fight to wean the poets away from any stirrings of African nationalist consciousness and to indoctrinate them with a universalist-individual outlook" (Chinweizu 197). Soyinka's "Abiku" is known for its treatment of individual freedom. This is at the expense of the rest of society. Poems such as Osundare's "Udoji" and Angira's "City plea: elegy of a Nationalist" are examples of the nationally set, non-universal, and non-individualistic new African poetry. The lyricism in Clark and Okigbo is perhaps linked to this individualism. As has been alerted at the beginning of this essay, some of these qualities attributed to the new poetry are seen as characteristic because of the intensity of their occurrence, unlike their absence or random occurrence in the earlier poetry.

The setting of these poems in the nation is a reflection of the audience-consciousness and a new radicalism which sees the country as the base for any socio-economic and political struggle for the well-being of the masses. Governments are generally held responsible for the neglect and exploitation of the common people and the exacerbating stratification of society into haves and have-nots. Thus the new poets are unabashedly local and they attempt to reach a particularized audience to talk to their compatriots. Clark and Soyinka seem to be addressing the whole world and humanity in *A Reed in the Tide* and *Idanre* respectively. However, didactic poetry as written by the new poets who are indebted to the African oral tradition is effective in a particularized setting as references, symbols, and images are reciprocally specific and relevant. The particularized setting has the advantage of poetic intensity and directness.

The concern for affairs of the nation does not preclude wider concerns in the new writing. Poets write on Africa, the Black world, and humanity. In *Songs of the Marketplace* there are "Soweto," "Namibia Talks," and "Zimbabwe." In addition, Osundare writes on Bob Marley, the late Jamaican reggae star. Funso Aiyejina in *Letter to Lynda and Other Poems* has poems on the West Indies. In *Labyrinths of the Delta* and *The Eagle's Vision* I write on Native Americans and African-Americans.

The national orientation of the new poetry is an admission that African problems now originate mainly from Africa and not from outside. This is a development in awareness of a trend which dates back to the second half of the 1960s. Even neocolonialism is seen now as working against the interests of African countries because of African collaborators, especially corrupt members of the ruling class. The new awareness has led to self-criticism. The new poets do not perceive themselves as an elite class but as part of the society in which and for which they write and criticise. Odia Ofeimun's *The Poet Lied* is an incisive critique of the role of the African poet. There is an indictment of the poet who is afraid of truth even at crucial times, when his speaking out should have been a moral weapon against forces of destruction. Such a poet's silence aligns him with oppressors. Osundare indicts the Nigerian University system to which he belongs in "Publish or Perish" and "At a University Con-Gre-Gation." He laments:

> O my people
> you stray
> seeking here
> a way across the wilderness   (29).

Contemporary African poetry is marked by a shift from culture, nature, individualism, and lyricism of the late 1950s and the early 1960s to the national socio-economic, political, and class awareness of the 1970s and 1980s. This shift in poetic materials and themes has a corresponding stylistic turn. There is movement away from Western modernist influences of fragmentation, allusiveness, and difficulty to the traditional African oratorical clarity and simplicity. The poetry is gradually "decolonised" in the shedding of the poetical in diction and syntax. There is also movement from the private self, the individualistic and the universal to the public and socially relevant. This by itself is movement from a non-political conservative stance to a radical ideological posture. There is a new nation-oriented, audience-conscious, rhetorical, and didactic poetry. The more defiant writers seem uninhibited by Western criticism of being overtly didactic and unartistic.

There is a new poetry with old ideas, values, and tastes changing to new ones. Historical happenings affecting ideas have placed their stamp on contemporary poetry in, for instance, placing the economic plight of the people over culture, discarding the universal for the immediate local, and perceiving Africans as mainly responsible for their problems. It is a poetry which has grown from an inchoate experimental stage to a more confident state, from eclecticism to authenticity, from stiff craftsmanship to a freer and more supple form. There is an increasing directness as images and materials are from an accessible environment. Sometimes it seems the generation has shed an earlier face for a new one, but because of the short history (from about 1960 to 1988) and because some of the older ones are publishing "new poetry," more recent than some of the younger ones who carry literary traits of the old, both groups belong to our time.

References and Works Cited

Achebe, Chinua. *Beware Soul Brother*. London: Heinemann, 1972.

Acholonu, Catherine. *The Spring's Last Drop*. Owerri: Totan, 1985.

Aiyejina, Funso. *Letter To Lynda and Other Poems*. Ife Monographs on Literature and Criticism,

Angira, Jared. *Silent Voices*. London: Heinemann, 1972.

———. *Cascades*. London: Longman, 1979.

Anyidoho, Kofi. *Elegy for the Revolution*. Greenfield Center, New York: Greenfield Review Press, 1978.

———. *A Harvest of Our Dreams*. London: Heinemann, 1984.

Awoonor, Kofi. *Rediscovery*. Ibadan: Mbari, 1964.

———. *Night of My Blood*. New York: Doubleday, 1971.

———. *Ride Me, Memory*. Greenfield Center, New York: Greenfield Review Press, 1973.

———. *The House By the Sea*. Greenfield Center, New York: Greenfield Review Press, 1978.

———. *The Morning After*. Accra: WOELI, 1987.

Bamikunle, Aderemi. "Review" of Ken Goodwin's *Understanding African Poetry* in *Saiwa*, Issue 3, 91.

Cheney-Coker, Syl. *The Graveyard Also Has Teeth with Concerto for an Exile*. London: Heinemann, 1980.

Chinweizu, Madubuike and Jemie. *Towards the Decolonization of African Literature*. New York/Lagos: NOK, 1980.

Clark-Bekederemo, J.P. *Poems*. Ibadan: Mbari, 1962.

———. *A Reed in the Tide*. London: Longman, 1965.

————. *Casualties*. London: Longman, 1971.

————. *A Decade of Tongues*. London: Longman, 1982.

————. *State of the Union*. London: Longman, 1985.

Eyi-Acquah, Kobena. *The Man Who Died*. Accra: Asempa, 1985.

Garuba, Harry. *Shadow and Dream*. Ibadan: New Horn, 1982.

Gibbs, James ed. *Critical Perspectives on Wole Soyinka*. Washington, DC: Three Continents, 1980.

Mapanje, Jack. *Of Chameleons and Gods*. London: Heinemann, 1981.

Nkosi, Lewis. *Tasks and Masks*. London: Longman, 1984.

Ofeimun, Odia. *The Poet Lied*. London: Longman, 1980.

————. *A Handle for the Flutist*. Lagos, 1987.

Ojaide, Tanure. *Children of Iroko & Other Poems*. Greenfield Center, New York: Greenfield Review Press, 1973.

————. *Labyrinths of the Delta*. Greenfield Center, New York: Greenfield Review Press, 1986.

————. *The Eagle's Vision*. Detroit: Lotus Press, 1987.

Okara, Gabriel. *The Fisherman's Invocation*. Benin City: Ethiope, 1978.

Okigbo, Christopher. *Labyrinths*. London: Heinemann, 1971.

Osundare, Niyi. *Songs of the Marketplace*. Ibadan: New Horn, 1983.

————. *Village Voices*. Ibadan: Evans, 1984.

————. *The Eye of the Earth*. Ibadan: Heinemann Nigeria, 1986.

————. *Moonsongs*. Ibadan: Spectrum, 1988.

p'Bitek, Okot. *Song of Lawino*. Nairobi: EAPH, 1966.

————. *Song of Ocol*. Nairobi: EAPH, 1967.

————. *Two Songs*. Nairobi: EAPH, 1971.

Peters, Lenrie. *Satellites*. London: Heinemann, 1967.

————. *Katchikali*. London: Heinemann, 1971.

————. *Selected Poetry*. London: Heinemann, 1981.

Soyinka, Wole. *Idanre and Other Poems*. London: Methuen, 1967.

————. *A Shuttle in the Crypt*. London: Rex Collings/Methuen, 1967.

————. *Ogun Abibiman*. London: Rex Collings, 1976.

————. *Mandela's Earth and Other Poems*. New York: Random House, 1988.

Ugah, Ada. *Naked Hearts*. Devon: Merlin Books, 1982.

————. *Songs of Talakawa*. Devon: Merlin Books, 1983.

6

New Trends in Modern African Poetry

Poetry in Africa is generally believed to be currently enjoying an unprecedented creative outburst and popularity. More and more people are taking their poetry writing seriously, many encouraged by poetry workshops. In addition to a wider readership of poetry books, large audiences attend reading sessions. Publicized prizes such as the Commonwealth Poetry Prize, the Noma Award, and the All-Africa Okigbo Prize for Poetry won by poets in recent years have exposed new African poetry and generated much interest in a branch of literature hitherto condemned as elitist, intellectual, difficult, and obscure.

The new popularity of poetry in Africa seems to also arise from the aptness of poetry as a succinct verbal art form in expressing feelings and attitudes in such economically desperate times as Africans have been going through. There is too the possibility of some aesthetic strength hitherto unrealized in written African poetry in the new works which have successfully adapted oral poetic techniques into the written form.

This topic presupposes an older tradition of modern African poetry, out of which writers have broken to write in new, albeit different, ways. The concept of what is old or new is relative in African literary history, bearing in mind that serious modern African poetry in English started only in the late 1950s. It was by the second half of the 1960s that most of the known modern African poets matured or established themselves as powerful voices. These, among others, include Christopher Okigbo, Wole Soyinka, J.P. Clark, Kofi Awoonor, Lenrie Peters, Okot p'Bitek and Dennis Brutus. These poets form a founding generation and consequently a tradition. However, before attempting to establish the watershed which gave rise to new African poetry, a few comments and acknowledgments.

Tradition and Novelty

There is the basic assumption generally of calling something recently discovered or noticed as new. In literature in particular, the old and the new can be rooted in the same tradition. Literature is after all a part of culture, which is a dynamic process. I have argued earlier that though written in European languages of English, French, and Portuguese, modern African literature cannot be English, French, or Portuguese; it carries African sensibility, culture, worldview, and response to their own peculiar reality.[1] By virtue of its shared experience as a people, the product of the African writer is different from those of other areas. Among African groups, literature has always been utilitarian. Thus much as I will attempt to point at new trends as opposed to old ones, it must be noted from the beginning that what new trends there are, are a development within the African people's tradition of poetry.

In every age artists struggle with their medium for relevance. In the course of this, they subconsciously or consciously attempt to re-define their aesthetics. The results of the struggle to find the necessary medium to articulate their ideas depend upon many factors, which their time and place impose on them. Relevance itself is a positive quality of art which contributes to its aesthetic distinction. Since experiences and responses to reality among a people may not be homogeneous because of individual, gender, class, and other prejudices, there are sometimes opposing and apparently contradictory trends in the same literary tradition. This variety is healthy for the arts as it leads like in a political pluralism to positive growth. I have chosen to deal with only English-speaking modern African poetry for my convenience.

The Problem of Publishing African Poetry

For a long time in the 1960s, African poetry was an exotic curiosity to the Western world of Europe and North America, and their multinational publishers such as Heinemann and Longman took keen interest in publishing African poets. Of course, the economies of African countries were far stronger then than they are now and Africans could buy books published abroad. The East African Publishing House did a good job between 1965 and 1973 before the demise of the East African Community and the economic disorientation brought about by the energy crisis. Today the multinational publishers, after their own restructuring as Heinemann went through in the early 1980s, publish very little African poetry. Heinemann is currently publishing two African books of poetry yearly. A few local publishers such as Woeli of Ghana, Baobab Books of Zimbabwe, New Horn, Malthouse, and Spectrum of Nigeria though energetic are constrained by economic realities to limit or suspend their poetry publications. Many poets are getting self-published as in the eastern part of Nigeria.

---

1. Tanure Ojaide, "Modern African Literature and Cultural Identity," Paper presented at the Centre for Asian and African Studies of El Colegio de Mexico, Mexico City, May 8, 1990, p. 2.

There is thus a diffusion of new works which are difficult to come by because of the lack of distributing experience of the small publishers. One hears of poets without seeing their works to read. In recent years the African Book Collective (ABC) based in Oxford, England, has been trying to distribute African books in the West. The full impact of the ABC is yet to be felt. Even the small presses in Britain and North America that publish African poets are unable to adequately expose new poets. The cost of books has become prohibitive in Africa and this is hampering both writing and publication.

Discussing new trends in modern African poetry therefore calls for a certain humility about the knowledge of what is recent in such rather commercially closed-in and economically depressed nationalities of the African cultural conglomeration. Such texts as *The Penguin Book of Modern African Poetry* (1984), Heinemann's *Summer Fires: New Poetry of Africa* (1983), *The Fate of Vultures: New Poetry of Africa* (1989), and *The Heinemann Book of African Poetry in English* (1991), and Malthouse's *Voices from the Fringe: An ANA Anthology of New Nigerian Poetry* (1988) are welcome consolations in the scanty literary bookscape.

The Historical Imperative

Africa's socio-political and economic history has a lot to do with the direction of writing in the continent. This point long made by Jaheinz Jahn and G-C. Mutiso is still valid of current African literature.[2] The period of nationalism immediately preceding and following political independence of most African countries between 1958 and 1963 was a time in which African writers were in an ecstatic mood. They wanted to exhibit and defend African culture against the Western rationalization of colonialism. The poets who were educated assumed the spokesmanship and cultural standard-bearing for their people and they seemed to have a foreign audience in mind. From the style of Okigbo, Soyinka, and Clark, among others of their generation, it seems they consciously wanted to prove themselves as fine poets and impress outsiders. As if form was an end in itself, there was over-emphasis on form at the expense of meaning. The poets of the 1960s were preoccupied with exhibiting African material culture and expressing their positions in a transition period. For many, it was in the context of culture conflict resulting from the choice to be made between traditional African culture

---

2. Jahn and Mutiso have expressed similar ideas in their respective earlier publications.

and the new Western culture. In the later 1960s and 1970s many poets were involved in political satire as the new African leaders generally failed the aspirations of their people.

Most of the poets went through universities like Legon (Ghana), Ibadan (Nigeria), and Makerere (Uganda) affiliated to and run in curriculum like British universities. In these schools, British professors fed African students with strong doses of modernist literature in the Departments of English. The modernist techniques of fragmentation, allusiveness, and obscurity imbibed in school did not enhance communication in the poetry of Soyinka in *Idanre and Other Poems* and Okigbo in both *Heavesgate* and *Limits*. J.P. Clark modelled such poems as "New Year" and "Ibadan Dawn" after Gerald Manley Hopkins, imitating the British poet's weird "sprung rhythm." Many of Soyinka's and Clark's poems were written in strict rhyme schemes. The European influence might also have been responsible for the nature and individualism expressed by the poets. The intellectual tastes of the time created and promoted by European Africanist critics such as Ulli Beier and Gerald Moore hailed this type of poetry.[3] While Okot p'Bitek is simple and Clark, Peters, and Awoonor are less difficult than Michael Echeruo, Soyinka, and early Okigbo, the generation seemed to have been seen more as difficult than more as varied.

By the mid-1970s the economic situation in most African countries had begun to deteriorate drastically. The leisurely rich times in which a Nigerian Head of State was quoted to have boasted that money was not his country's problem but how to spend it were over.[4] The new harsh times brought issues of physical survival. Many African countries had been or were still involved in civil wars, which consumed their human and natural resources. Things were socially not the same again in Nigeria after the civil war. At this time the African middle-class to which virtually all the established poets belonged started to be radicalized. By March 1978 when there was the conference on "Radical Perspectives on African Literature" at Ibadan, there was sharp polarization of the intelligentsia between radicals and conservatives.

A certain notion had begun to gain ground among young writers and critics that the African writer *has* to be an instrument of change, more so in periods when the generality of the populace had become economically and politically marginalised. Almost concurrently there were calls for the decolonization of African literature with Chinweizu a major

---

3. Ulli Beier praises Okigbo's musicality in "Three Mbari Poets," *Black Orpheus*, 12 (1963).

4. Yakubu Gowon, the Nigerian leader between 1966 and 1975 is said to have made such remarks.

voice. The intellectual tastes have begun to change, giving way to new aesthetic conditioning for poets.

New trends in modern African poetry are a development from and yet a deliberate reaction against earlier trends, especially those associated with early Okigbo, Soyinka, and Clark. As I have also written, the younger poets who are highly educated and exposed are not as self-conscious as their predecessors. While they respect the older poets, they seem to reject their conservative poetic practices which are too formal and imitative of Western poetic tradition (Ojaide 116).

There started in the 1970s a strong trend to decolonise African poetry. Thus while one can fairly easily point out the influences of Eliot and Pound on Okigbo, of Hopkins on Clark, and Shakespeareanisms in Soyinka, most poems written since about 1973 seem to have shed foreign influences. I must quickly point out too that the decolonization process in recent African poetry is done in diverse ways as the aesthetic conceptions of individuals. It is pertinent to note too that the current of change in poetry has swept old as well as young practitioners. Thus as will be seen in the course of this essay, established older poets as Kwesi Brew, Kofi Awoonor, Lenrie Peters, J.P. Clark, and Wole Soyinka have published new works since the mid-1970s and in fact the latter two have their latest poetry works published in 1988.[5]

The Consequences of Socio-Economic Hardships

A major trend in recent modern African poetry emanates from the dire economic predicament of most African countries, which has exposed more than before the intolerable gap between the rich and the poor, the haves and the have-nots. Almost all the poets have taken positions to the left of center and some like Niyi Osundare, Ada Ugah, and Jared Angira once declared themselves Marxists. These poets and others have written poems which deal with the plight of the common people, peasants, and workers, from their ideological perspectives. Syl Cheney-Coker's "Peasants," Jared Angira's "Quiet oratorio" and "Obbligato from the public gallery," much of Ugah's *Songs of Talakawa*, Osundare's *Songs of the Marketplace* and a few poems in *Moonsongs* appear to be in this masses-oriented, ideologically informed vein.

It has looked more fashionable among poets from the mid-1970s more than before to align with the economically exploited, underprivi-

---

5. J.P. Clark, *Mandela and Other Poems* (Ikeja: Longman Nigeria, 1988) and Wole Soyinka, *Mandela's Earth and Other Poems* (New York: Random House, 1988).

leged masses of the society. Clark's *State of the Union* falls into this trend. The poetry of this inspiration tends to sound propagandistic, highly rhetorical, stridently passionate, and very audience-conscious. Success depends upon the maturity and special talent of the individual poet. If the poets' aim is to generate revulsion for the privileged and exploiters and sympathy for their victims, they generally succeed. Whether it is Osundare talking about Ikoyi and Ajegunle in *Moonsongs* or Clark's "Victoria Island Re-visited" in *State of the Union*, poets have of recent been preoccupied with mundane, real socio-economic problems of the society. This is a generation away from the speculative abstractions of the early 1960s as in the "lonely figure" and "grey seasons" sections of Soyinka's *Idanre and Other Poems*.

The poets are now using their art as a means of attempting to reverse the negative socio-economic order in their societies so that economic equality and justice will prevail. Theirs is a new kind of humanism arising from the human suffering resultant from African debt-sagged economies. Though commitment in African writing has always been peddled at one time or another, there seems borne out by thematic and technical preoccupations in much of recent African poetry a strong commitment towards socio-economic change for the benefit of the generality of the people. It is a poetry whose function is geared towards socio-economic liberation.

Search for Political Alternatives

Running concurrently with, and sometimes inseparable from, the socio-economic problem is the theme of political corruption which involves tyranny, despotism, and economic mismanagement. The poets blame the political leaders for the economic demise of their countries because of their spendthrift habit. Such is the image portrayed in "The Fate of Vultures" where

> The chief and his council, a flock of flukes
> gambolling in the veins of fortune.
> Range chickens, they consume and scatter;
> they ran for a pocket-lift
> in the corridors of power
> and shared contracts in cabals—
> the record produce and sales
> fuelled the adolescent bonfire of fathers   (Ojaide 11).

Less veiled is Soyinka's "The Apotheosis of Master-Sergeant Doe," in which there is a strong indictment of the "Master slayer" that his people need to be redeemed from.

Malawian poets in particular have written against tyranny and despotism in their country. Blood, wounds, and torture are common features in Frank Chipasula's poems. Titles such as "A Hanging," "The Hangman," "The Blind Marimba Player," and "Because the Wind Remembers" tell the sordid tale of the physical and psychological brutalization unleashed by the Banda leadership in Malawi. Jack Mapanje in *Of Chameleons and Gods* is more veiled and subtle than Chipasula in *O Earth, Wait for Me* and *Whispers in Wings*.

In all cases, the poets tend to use wit, irony, sarcasm, antithesis, and repulsive imagery to express their disgust and contempt for the corruption and tyranny of those they criticize. Chipasula says: "they hail him Messiah, Saviour / as he fattens on larceny" (37). Soyinka dismisses the Master-Sergeant as "The ass that mimes the Lord's anointed" (33). Such leaders are seen as so contemptible that "when they die, of course, only their kind / shower praises on vultures" (Ojaide (11). As long as most African leaders continue to plague their people, so will this trend continue.

Hope in a Bleak Landscape

A correlative of prevailing economic hardship and political misrule is the overwhelmingly bleak atmosphere created in recent African poetry. In a review of *The Fate of Vultures* in the *ANA Review '89*, Femi Shaka writes:

> The recently published BBC Prize-winning poetry, *The Fate of Vultures*, perhaps confirms a long suspected trend in contemporary African poetry, towards the employment of images that grant little room for optimism in the ever-increasing voices of lettered men...The unusual longing for a surfeit of gloomy imagery, and the bloodied language was first noticed in a recent collection of young Nigerian poets...
>
> One needed some kind of continental representative of this paradigm to be able to make valid judgments. With the publication, *The Fate of Vultures*, this trend toward gloomy imagery proves not unique to Nigeria but is a continental phenomenon (13).

He cites as examples of such gloomy poems the title/prize-winning poem, Tanure Ojaide's "The Fate of Vultures," Esiaba Irobi's "Nectars," Gichora Mwangi's "If," and others, ranging from West through East to North Africa to corroborate his claim of a pessimistic trend. In "Morbid Landscape, Morbid Lines," E. Ogaga Ifowodo finds the poets only reflecting the bleak African reality, a trend which as far back as the mid-1960s was presaged by Okigbo in a lament:

> The wailing is for the fields of crop
> The drum's lament is

> They grow not...
> The wailing is for the fields of crop
> For the barren wedded ones
> For perishing children
> The wailing is for the great river
> Her pot-bellied watchers
> Despoil her...   (50).

As Ifowodo points out, the harsh economic measures of both the IMF and the World Bank have aggravated the African plight gradually leading the continent into one "bland sheet of pain and agony" (13).

Poets tend to reflect the prevailing reality of their times; they live the reality which is imposed on them from outside by time and space. Thus they do not invent their own reality and if Africa of the past one and a half decades is in a miserable plight, their response to reality will show this unpleasant state. However, depending upon their peculiar insights, they project a vision into the future which may be in consonance with their wishes. Thus strong as the trend of the "African nightmare," many poets project hope.

Examples from *The Fate of Vultures* and other works are copious. Even in the so-called pessimistic poems of the BBC African poetry anthology, Ifowodo sees the declaration: "I would not follow the hurricane / nor would I the whirlwind / in their brazen sweep away; / they leave misery in their wake" and Afam Akeh's soul lighting up "the dark / with its lustrous craving for nectar" as being anchored on sturdy hope (13). In *Labyrinths of the Delta* the poet projects a vision of salvation:

> People look towards the arrival
> there are many stars in the horizon
> in every heart grows the curative herb
> the maiden smiles in the throes of labour
> she smiles in the shadow of another age
> the shadow drenched by regenerating hormones   (Ojaide 102).

Of course, there are celebrations as in love, an area I will deal with later in this essay. While conscious of the bleak present, many poets project hope of better times into the African future.

Movement Towards National Literatures

Another major new trend in modern African poetry is the focusing of the poets on national experiences as never before. Unlike in the 1960s when the poets were culturally obsessed, nature-oriented and "universal," today old and young poets are addressing their national issues more aggressively than before. Though Okigbo, Clark, and Soyinka all responded to the Nigerian crisis of the late 1960s and though Okot p'Bitek touched upon the Ugandan political situation of the post-independence period, they did so from a general African and human perspective. With the excesses of political independence, the poets have come to believe that Africans are mainly responsible for their problems. In their desire to effect changes, they use the nation-state as the starting point.

The poets are very particularized in their treatment of problems peculiar to their countries. Somehow they seem to be questioning themselves and other Africans as never before what it means to be African. The solidarity of black peoples in exhibiting culture as in the 1950s, 1960s, and 1970s has been eroded and the poets are cultivating new constituencies of readership. Thus poets from The Gambia, Sierra Leone, Ghana, Nigeria, Kenya, Malawi, Zimbabwe, and South Africa are creating national literatures, making it more plausible now to talk about an individual nation's poetry as was not the case before the mid-1970s.

Turning inward, the poets "speak the truth / about ourselves to ourselves" (Ojaide 1987:1). They attempt to criticize the deficiencies of their countries like betrayed lovers. Tijan M. Sallah, for instance, critically "surveys the Gambian landscape" (1). In "A Love Poem for My Country," the Malawian Chipasula writes:

> I have nothing to give you, but my anger
> And the filaments of my hatred reach across the border
> You, you have sold many and me to exile....
>
> Your streets are littered with handcuffed men
> And the drums are thuds of the warden's spiked boots.
> You wriggle with agony as the terrible twins, law and order,
> Call out the tune through the thick tunnel of barbed wire (39).

This is a strong indictment of Kamuzu Banda's tyrannical administration. Jack Mapanje's *Of Chameleons and Gods* uses Malawian mythology to make critical statements on the same regime. This patriotic gesture is ironically taken to be a treasonable act by the sell-out rulers.

Similarly, many Nigerian and Ghanaian poets criticize the state of their countries. Osundare has the Nigerian scene in mind in the "Songs of Home and Around" section of *Songs of the Marketplace*. In the XXII segment of *Moonsongs*, the poet uses two contrasting sections of Lagos to convey the wide gap between the Nigerian haves and have-nots:

> Ikoyi
>> The moon here
>> is a laundered lawn

> its grass the softness of infant fluff;
> silence gazes like a joyous lamb,
> doors romp on lazy hinges
> the ceiling is a sky
> weighted down by chandeliers
> of pampered stars

Ajegunle
> here the moon
> is a jungle,
> sad like a forgotten beard
> with tensioned climbers
> and undergrowths of cancerous fury:
> cobras of anger spit in every brook
> and nights are one long prowl
> of swindled leopards   (42).

Silas Obadiah, a young Nigerian poet, is disappointed at the course of events in Nigeria. He asks:

> Was it ever heard here brothers
> That the soldier's gun-shot left no victims?
> Has any leader's sword ever returned to its sheath unstained?
> Or has any chief ever emptied his flowing barns to assuage any
>   famine?   (qtd. in Garuba 119).

Clark's *State of the Union* is a critique of the Nigerian state. Soyinka's "My Tongue Does Not Marry Slogans" in *Mandela's Earth*, Tunde Fatoba's poems, Ezenwa-Ohaeto's *I Wan Be General*, and many of Ojaide's poems in *Labyrinths of the Delta* and *The Eagle's Vision* have as a backdrop the Nigerian society.

In the same manner, Kofi Awoonor's *The House by the Sea* and Kofi Anyidoho's *Elegy for the Revolution* and *Earthchild* are based on their particularized Ghanaian experiences. The poets love their countries but criticize the administrations in power and also look forward, like Chipasula, to a day that will "wash away my pain / And I will emerge from the night breaking into song / Like the sun, blowing out these evil stars" (5–6).

There is a lot of personification in the poetry which deals with individual countries. Mainly it is political satire. As a result of the particularized focus, there are topical allusions which are better understood by those sharing the same historical and social background. There are to be found in this national poetry passion and concreteness.

Apart from national focus and trends, there are regional characteristics that are observable in West African and East and Central African poets. Malawian and Zimbabwean poets, including Jack Mapanje,

Felix Mnthali and Musaemura Bonas Zimunya tend to be more descriptive of physical landscapes. West African poets, especially in Nigeria and Ghana, are linguistic iconoclasts. The reasons for the regional difference are similar to national difference as the defunct East African Community and the Economic Community of West African States were conceived to bring the peoples of the respective sub-regions together.

Self-criticism

Self-criticism is a strong trend in West African poetry. As poets become "very true to ourselves," there is increasing self-analysis and criticism. This goes beyond poets criticizing corrupt leaders to criticizing their middle class, university ivory tower status. Odia Ofeimun seemed to have started this literary trail with *The Poet Lied* (1980) in which he criticizes a poet who appeared to him not to have supported the cause of truth in such a critical period as that of the Nigerian civil war. Osundare in *Songs of the Marketplace* lashes at the University establishment:

O my people
you stray
seeking here
a way across the wilderness   (29).

Soyinka's "My Tongue Does Not Marry Slogans" also lashes at the academic community, who though most vocal and left-oriented are themselves guilty of the accusations of corruption they level against others. For instance,

Midnight missed you at the barricades
But found you snoring sweetly in your mistress's
Arms, secured by campus walls, manned
Day and night by "wage-slave proletarians"   (54).

This is a strong indictment of the hypocrisy of university faculty who do not practice what they preach and use their so-called academic freedom to misbehave. This questioning of class and the role of the poet is meant to destroy assumptions that one has an alternative vision for society because one is a poet. The individual's integrity is important and the privilege of being a poet or an academician in an underdeveloped country does not remove one from the standards set for society at large.

Content and Meaning

African poets from the 1970s have continued to pay more attention to content and meaning than was done before then. There are many factors responsible for the prevailing development of trying to communicate ideas and feelings clearly. Since the poets deal with mainly public themes rather than private ones, there is a correlating shift in style to a public voice. There is also the pressure to communicate urgently the desperate socio-economic and political situation that needs to be rectified. In addition, the poets have become more audience-conscious because of poetry workshops and other avenues and the increasing importance of "secondary orality" through the television and radio.

Quite unlike the stilted and pedantic voice in either early Clark or Soyinka as in *Idanre and other Poems*, there is a new discursive unpretentiously clear voice with almost the syntax of prose. The strength of a poem has come to be seen as being more in the sharpness of the images and the subtlety and wit of expression rather than in difficult language.

Unlike in the late 1950s, 1960s, and early 1970s when Western modernist influences were strong, in their desire to be more culturally relevant, African poets from the mid-1970s have turned to use indigenous African poetic techniques. Angus Calder, Jack Mapanje, and Cosmo Pieterse introducing *Summer Fires: New Poetry of Africa* observe that "many authors are clearly influenced by oral tradition, which made their work specially suitable for broadcasting" (x). There is a general recourse of old and younger poets to oral poetry techniques.

There appears to be "a symbiotic relationship between the oral and the written in modern West African poetry in which the poetic aim, vision, and practice have fused to produce a poetry that is distinctly oral though written. Modern West African poets, especially the younger ones desirous of large audiences, are adapting their poetic techniques to the growing influence of broadcast media and public performance."[6] J. Apronti talks of the poetry recital theatre set up in Ghana in the 1970s which attracts people from all walks of life and permanently projects poetry as a public event (Ogungbesan 31–34). In Nigeria there are poetry readings in the Universities of Ibadan, Ife, Lagos, Maiduguri, Nsukka, and Zaria. For a long time in the late 1970s and in the 1980s there was a strong writers' workshop at Chancellor College, Zomba (Malawi), which Jack Mapanje and Felix Mnthali participated in.

The language of recent African poetry taking a cue from traditional poetry aims at clarity of expression. As I have mentioned earlier, the poets use simple language to match their concern for the common people. According to Osundare in his *Songs of the Marketplace*, "Poetry is

---

6. Tanure Ojaide, "Orality in Recent West African Poetry," Paper presented at the University of Calabar Conference on African Literature and the English Language, 1988, p. 2.

/ no oracle's kernel / for a sole philosopher's stone" but "man meaning / to / man" (1–2). Lenrie Peters in his "new poems," Soyinka in *Madela's Earth*, Clark in both *State of the Union* and *Mandela*, Osundare in *Village Voices*, *Songs of the Marketplace* and *The Eye of the Earth*, and Kofi Anyidoho in *A Harvest of Our Dreams*, among others, have clarity of expression and directness of address as in traditional African poetry. Traditional oratory and rhetoric in the form of proverbs, praisenames, axioms, and idiomatic expressions have been imbibed. Examples are rife in *The Eye of the Earth* and *Earthchild*. The effect of this recent trend of turning to indigenous poetic techniques and imbibing oral features is to make African poetry more accessible, more directly related to African cultures, and more popular.

Two changes in poetic practice are related to the use of oral poetry features. One has to do with repetitions and musicality. Poets like Okigbo, Soyinka, and Clark were very musical in their poetry of the 1960s. Okigbo admits being inspired by Western classical composers (qtd. in Pieterse 133). Okigbo sometimes gives the impression of being carried away by the musicality of words at the expense of meaning as in:

> For we are listening in cornfields
>   among the windplayers,
> listening to the wind leaning over
>   its loveliest fragment   (5).

Repetitions then were mainly to enhance musicality. Clark attempted to create "sprung rhythm" with his repetitions. Soyinka's excessive alliterations in "The Dreamer," "To My First White Hairs," and "Malediction" are great impediments to comprehension.

African poets, including the older ones, in recent years as in the traditional African context "find meaning more important than music, which is supposed to be a non-distracting accompaniment" (Ojaide 116). Repetitions now "are more for emphasis and mnemonic effects than for musicality. The musicality is incidental" (Ojaide 116).

The other change has to do with the use made of African culture. Once it was the material culture which was important as writers wanted to sell it to the outside world. Ironically, while displaying traditional African ways of life, many of the poets used alien poetic techniques as has been adequately illustrated. However, material culture is no longer taken too seriously and the writers are taking up cultural poetic techniques of parallelism, topicality, indirectness, repetition, and others to express their contemporary feelings.

Formal Experimentation

A loosening and diversification of form has emerged as a major trend in contemporary African poetry. Contrary to Ken Goodwin who puts down the new African poetry as lacking craft compared to the poetry of the 1960s,[7] I strongly feel that the poetic form in Africa today has become more relaxed, flexible, diversified, and indigenized as to confuse a critic used to British and Western forms.

Poets have increasingly made use of traditional poetic forms, which for them have a cultural validation. Harry Garuba writes on "four folk figures" in *Shadows and Dream*. Similarly, Osundare and Soyinka exploit the Yoruba *oriki* and *ijala* traditional chant forms in their poetry. Osundare's "Earth" in *The Eye of the Earth* is like an extended praise-name:

> Temporary basement
> and lasting roof
>
> first clayey coyness
> and last alluvial joy
>
> breadbasket
> and compost bed...   (1).

In "Muhammad Ali at the Ringside, 1985," Soyinka uses traditional Yoruba praise-chant style to describe Ali's dexterity in the boxing ring:

> Black tarantula whose antics hypnotize the foe!
> Butterfly sideslipping death from rocket probes.
> Bee whose sting, unsheathed, picks the teeth
> Of the raging hippopotamus, then fans
> The jaw's convergence with its flighty wings.
> Needle that threads the snapping fangs
> Of crocodiles, knots the tusks of elephants
> On rampage. Cricket that claps and chirrups
> Round the flailing horn of the rhinoceros,
> Then shuffles, does a bugalloo, tap-dances on its tip.
> Space that yields, then drowns the intruder....
> Esu with faces turned to all four compass points
> Astride a weather vane; they sought to trap him,
> Slapped the wind each time   (48).

This shift in Soyinka started in *Ogun Abibiman* (1976).

---

7. Quoted by Aderemi Bamikunle in a review of Ken Goodwin's *Understanding African Poetry* in *Saiwa*, Issue 3, p. 91.

There are more examples of the strong presence of indigenous forms. Okimba Launko (Femi Osofisan) uses a traditional praying form in his "Blessings." Anyidoho uses Chorus and Invocation in the highly dramatic "In the High Court of Cosmic Justice." In the same Anyidoho's *Earthchild* there are fine examples of the praise-name formula in written poetry:

> Adonu Adokli
> Dancer-Extraordinary
> who threw dust into Master-drummer's eyes,
> Asase Yaa,
> Sustainer of fertile soil and womb....
> Olokun,
> Supreme Commander of unruly seas....
> Old Shango,
> Controller-General of light and sounded flame....
> Nene Ani,
> Mother-Queen of Earth...   (76).

Tanure Ojaide has attempted to use the curse, abuse, and lamentation forms in *The Eagle's Vision*. "The Evidence of the Hyena" and "For the Sell-Out" are meant to be curses, while "The Outcast" is modelled on an Urhobo mockery form. The use of indigenous forms has made the poems more dramatic and lively and given new African poetry its own uniqueness despite being written in English or other European languages.

Varieties of Language

Though the African poets I am dealing with generally write in English, there has developed a trend which deserves attention. More and more writers are mixing their African languages with English and an increasing number writing in pidgin English. These two movements are very strong especially in Ghana and Nigeria, both in West Africa.

Atukwei Okai, Kojo Laing, Kobena Eyi-Acquah, Niyi Osundare, Femi Osofisan, and Soyinka are prominent in interlacing English with their local languages. In Laing's *Godhorse* (1989), many Akan words which have entered popular Ghanaian English slang are frequently used and poems such as "Godsdoor" and "I am the freshly dead husband" are examples of an Akan-suffused English. In other cases, lines in indigenous languages serve as refrains. This again particularizes the audience and reaches the not-too-educated more than it would if written in very intellectual language. The audience from the same language area tends to identify more with the poet, who is propagating his or her culture.

A closely related phenomenon is that in order to match their ideological commitment, many poets especially in Nigeria have for the past decade begun to use pidgin English seriously. Frank Aig-Imoukhuede has written many pidgin poems. Mamman Vatsa, the Nigerian soldier-poet, Tunde Fatoba, and Ezenwa-Ohaeto have been chief users of pidgin English. This definitely has extended their audience to include those who are not too literate. The vogue of pidgin English poetry is to bring poetry to the African masses by de-emphasizing its intellectualism. Poems in pidgin English express serious and profound ideas in a rather light-hearted language and when the poems succeed as in Ezenwa-Ohaeto's *Song of Traveller* and *I wan be General*, they are a blend of wit, humor, unconventional imagery, play on words and sound, and accessible allusions to achieve effective communication.

Generation Gap

It is normal as in Africa to have three 'generations' of writers: the Soyinka-Clark-Awoonor-Peters older group, the middle group of Anyidoho-Chipasula-Ojaide-Osundare group, and the very young group represented in *Voices from the Fringe*. However, there is another generational factor in African poetry which has to do with the wider social behavior. This trend seems to be a development from the culture conflict theme of the late 1950s and the 1960s. Each generation appears uncomfortable with the other.

The younger generation seems contemptuous of the old because of its inability to change. Other younger ones see themselves as falling short of the discipline, courage, and achievements of their elders. There are also others who ridicule this view and feel they have gone beyond the achievements of their parents. Tijan M. Sallah conveys these conflicting views in "Generations:"

> In my father's house
> We eat with brown fingers.
> Grandma licks her slender fingers;
> Aunt Bintu chews the chicken bones.
>
> In my father's house,
> We spoon our mouths with silver.
> Mother forks the half-cooked mutton,
> And brother Mawdo knifes the soft cassava.
>
> In my house, I prefer
> The dark, raw road of my grandpa.
> But my children branch—

One follows fingers and mats.
The other spoons and tablecloths   (31).

The conflict between the individual and his or her parents is expressed in many poems of *The Endless Song*. In "I will take you to the mountain," the speaker of the poem tells a parent-figure:

Your mountain has sunk below our minds,
and we need not hunt the beasts
we have tamed with generosity.
Do not think we are not warriors because we do not
wield matchets in our daily circles—
we can be heroes without spilling blood   (16).

At the same time, the poet feels he is "not the true son / of whose story" he tells (19). Jack Mapanje's "The New Platform Dances" is an expression of the loss of the cultural energy and vitality through Western education. However, in "These Too Are Our Elders" the poet asks, "Why do these elders always exploit our disbelief?" The questioning of generational values is a continuing process and will always be pursued in African poetry.

The Rise of Female Voices

While poetry appears to be the commonest literary mode for self-expression and is thriving well these days, women have not made a strong mark in the poetry scene, unlike their achievements in fiction and drama. However, there is a growing number of women poets, some recently published whose works have been under-exposed. The works of three Nigerian women poets published in the later 1980s deserve attention: Mabel Segun's *Conflict and Other Poems* (1986), Molara Ogundipe-Leslie's *Sew the Old Days* (1986), and Catherine Acholonu's *The Spring's Last Drop* (1985) and *Nigeria in the Year 1999 and Other Poems* (1985).

Mabel Segun in "The Smart One" and "Corruption" deals with the social malaise of her Nigerian society. Funso Aiyejina says her poetry is "accessible and direct without being simplistic and she is an effective user of irony and macabre humour" (qtd. in Otukunefor and Nwodo 137). Ogundipe-Leslie appears to be the most radical of the three women poets, Marxist-inclined. She is also a feminist as her "Yoruba Love" shows. Occasionally she is highly intellectual and Maduakor sees her in "Those Rags...My Rags of Time" "at her most metaphysical (ingenious) moment" (qtd. in Otukunefore and Nwodo 84).

The younger Catherine Acholonu is more of a traditionalist. In "The Spring's Last Drop" she goes up the hill overcoming the distractions of modern life to fetch "the spring's last drop" for her children:

> I Obianuju
> I shall provide my children
> with plenty
> I shall multiply this drop
> they will never taste
> of the wasting fluid
> of the sea   ·   (17).

Reinforcing her acceptance of the traditional role of responsible mother-hood, "Lost Virtue" laments the emergence of the modern woman. The poet is strongly rooted in tradition which is manifested in her role as mother and priestess and her being anchored on her father and hus-band. Unlike the feminist Ogundipe-Leslie, Acholonu is a womanist ac-cepting the tradition which to say the least has kept women as posses-sions of men.

The sheer number of women poets included in *Voices from the Fringe: An ANA Anthology of New Nigerian Poetry* is an indication of the creative ferment going on among women poets in Africa. Juliet Amokiese, Betty Ezemba, Ogechi Ezemba, Olufunmilayo Jibowu, Nana Aishatu Magaji, Nina Unigwe, Chinwe Esiaba, and Phanuel Egejuru are the tip of the iceberg of women's poetic output in Africa. As women get liberated, get equal opportunities in education, are less-overburdened by housekeeping and mothering, and have a stronger sense of self-realization, more of them will write poems to express their feelings.

Love Poetry

"Love poems," according to Obi Maduakor, "are a rare species in African poetry" (qtd. in Okunefor and Nwodo 77). This has not been so since the 1980s. With Kobena Eyi-Acquah's *The Man Who Died* (1984), Okimba Launko's *Minted Coins* (1987), Esiaba Irobi's "Soniya" and Tanure Ojaide's *Labyrinths of the Delta* (1986) and *The Endless Song* (1989), there is a strong current of African love po-etry often ignored by critics. Somewhere along the line, modern African poets were so overwhelmed with culture and later with socio-economic issues that they failed to carry on the indigenous tra-dition of love songs. The speaker in Launko's "Love's Discotheque" tells his love:

> in other women, my lady,
> just a banal ritual of dressing
> but you turn such things to symphony...
> & I can only dance along   (20).

"Queen" in the same collection is also a powerful expression of the poet's love for a woman. Love portrayed in African poetry tends to be subtle, indirect, and never obscene.

Conclusion

I have attempted to expose the current trends in themes, techniques, and formal issues in African poetry. Traits of old trends have not totally been shed. For example, Sallah's *Koraland* takes one back to the 1960s when displaying material culture was in vogue. Osundare's use of alliteration in *The Eye of the Earth* is similar to Okigbo's and Soyinka's in *Heavensgate* and *Idanre* respectively. Some of the new trends were scantily showing in old days but are more emphasiz*ed now*. Okot p'Bitek in first writing in Acoli before translating *Song of Lawino* to English made use of traditional African poetic techniques. However, his example was not the fashion in his time.

Modern African poetry has never been so vibrant and varied. There are multiple trends, some conflicting. In many poets the national and human and the personal and public concerns do not exclude one another. There is tension in the conflict of allegiance between one's immediate national society and the larger world. The focus is on the nation, the continent, the race, and class. Each of these units is subsisted by a sense of humanity.

There are indications that despite the demise of communism in Eastern Europe and the flowering of multi-party politics in Africa and the gradual dismantling of apartheid in South Africa, African poetry will continue to be radical. This is because of the debt burden created by the IMF and the World Bank and the worsening socio-economic plight of African countries. Thus even though the ideological point has been blunted in international politics, there will still be strident calls for the amelioration of the plight of the abused masses. Poets will continue to portray the bleak socio-economic landscape with negative and ugly images and dream of light at the end of the tunnel.

As one will expect, there will be more women poets as more of them get educated and realise themselves. These women poets might begin to focus on their femaleness and in the process gender will play an important role in African poetry as it now does in African-American fiction. As people get less inhibited by traditional taboos, there will be more of love poetry.

Experiments in form will intensify. Currently there are attempts to write more co-ordinated long poems. This trend will be taken up by many poets who feel mature and confident enough to take risks in form to achieve greatness. There will be more of the subsuming of indigenous oral poetic forms into writing that will be distinctly African. As poets widen their readership, more oral literature techniques will be adopted. Living through the same times of political inefficiency and economic hardship, the poets express about the same concerns.

Still, there is a variety. There are also degrees of, for instance, radicalism and commitment. The new trends are strongest as they relate to themes, radical viewpoint, language, and form. Each trend has its own artistic validity in the circumstances in which the poems are written. There are some trends which because I am myself involved in and too close to in time that I may be blinded from noticing. What is remarkable though is the vibrant expressive spirit trying to capture in succinct images, language, and inherited forms the current reality of Africans and the perennial human condition.

Works Cited

Acholonu, Catherine. *The Spring's Last Drop*. Owerri: Totan, 1985.

———. *Nigeria in the Year 1999 and Other Poems*. Owerri: Totan, 1985.

Angira, Jared. *Silent Voices*. London: Heinemann, 1972.

———. *Cascades*. London: Heinemann, 1979.

Anyidoho, Kofi. *Elegy for the Revolution*. New York: Greenfield Review Press, 1978.

———. *A Harvest of our Dreams*. London: Heinemann, 1984.

———. *Earthchild*. Legon: Woeli, 1985.

Awoonor, Kofi. *The House By The Sea*. New York: Greenfield Review Press, 1978.

———. *Until the Morning After*. New York: Greenfield Review Press, 1987.

Busia, Abena, P. A. *Testimonies of Exile*. Trenton, New Jersey: AWP, 1990.

Calder, Angus with Jack Mapanje and Cosmo Pieterse, eds. *Summer Fires: New Poetry of Africa*. London: Heinemann, 1983.

Cheney-Coker, Syl. *The Graveyard Also Has Teeth with Concerto for an Exile*. London: Heinemann, 1980.

Chinweizu, Onwuchekwa Jemie and Ihechukwu Madubuike. *Toward the Decolonization of African Literature*. Enugu: Fourth Dimension, 1980.

Chipasula, Frank. *O Earth, Wait for Me*. Braamfontein: Raven Press1984.

———. *Whispers in the Wings*. Oxford: Heinemann, 1991.

Clark, J.P. *A Decade of Tongues*. London: Longman, 1982.

———. *State of the Union*. London: Longman, 1985.

———. *Mandela and Other Poems*. London: Longman, 1988.

Eyi-Acquah, Kobena. *The Man Who Died*. Accra: Asempa, 1985.

Ezenwa-Ohaeto, *Song of Traveller*. Awka: Towncrier, 1986.

Garuba, Harry. *Shadow and Dream*. Ibadan: New Horn, 1982.

———. ed. *Voices from the Fringe: An ANA Anthology of New Nigerian Poetry*. Lagos: Malthouse, 1988.

Goodwin, Ken. *Understanding African Poetry: A Study of Ten Poets*. London: Heinemann, 1982.

Jahn, Janheinz. *Neo-African Literature: A History of Black Writing*. New York: Grove, 1961.

Laing, Kojo. *Godhorse*. Oxford: Heinemann, 1989.

Launko, Okimba. *Minted Coins*. Ibadan: Heinemann Nigeria, 1987.

Mapanje, Jack. *Of Chameleons and Gods*. London: Heinemann, 1981.

Moore, Gerald and Ulli Beier. *The Penguin Book of Modern African Poetry*. Harmondsworth: Penguin, 1984.

Mutiso, Gideon-Cyrus Makau. *Socio-Political Thought in African Literature*. New York: Barnes and Noble, 1974.

Ofeimun, Odia. *The Poet Lied*. London: Longman, 1980.

———. *A Handle for the Flutist*. Lagos, 1987.

Ogungbesan, Kolawole. ed. *New West African Literature*. London: Heinemann, 1979.

Ogundipe-Leslie, Molara. *Sew the Old Days*. Ibadan: Evans, 1985.

Ojaide, Tanure. *Children of Iroko & Other Poems*. New York: Greenfield Review Press, 1973.

———. *Labyrinths of the Delta*. New York: Greenfield Review Press, 1986.

———. *The Eagle's Vision*. Detroit: Lotus Press, 1987.

———. *The Endless Song*. Lagos: Malthouse, 1989.

———. "The Changing Voice of History: Contemporary African Poetry," *Geneve-Afrique*, vol. XXVII, no 1 (1989).

———. *The Fate of Vultures*. Lagos: Malthouse, 1990.

———. *The Blood of Peace*. Oxford: Heinemann, 1991.

Okigbo, Christopher. *Labyrinths*. London: Heinemann, 1971.

Osofisan, Femi (Okimba Launko). *Minted Coins*. Ibadan: Heinemann, 1987.

Osofisan, Femi et al. eds. *ANA Review: Annual Journal of the Association of Nigerian Authors*. Vol. 4, no. 6 (November 1989).

Osundare, Niyi. *Songs of the Marketplace*. Ibadan: New Horn, 1983.

———. *Village Voices*. Ibadan: Evans, 1984.

———. *The Eye of the Earth*. Ibadan: Heinemann Nigeria, 1986.

———. *Moonsongs*. Ibadan: Spectrum, 1988.

———. *Waiting Laughters*. Lagos: Malthouse, 1990.

p'Bitek, Okot. *Song of Lawino*. Nairobi: EAPH, 1966.

Peters, Lenrie. *Selected Poetry*. London: Heinemann, 1981.

Sallah, Tijan M. *Koraland*. Washington, DC: Three Continents Press, 1989.

————. *Dreams of Dusty Roads*. Washington, DC: Three Continents, 1993.

Segun, Mabel. *Conflict and Other Poems*. Ibadan: New Horn, 1986.

Soyinka, Wole. *Idanre and Other Poems*. London: Methuen, 1967.

————. *A Shuttle in the Crypt*. London: Rex Collings/Methuen, 1972.

————. *Ogun Abibiman*. London: Rex Collings, 1976.

————. *Mandela's Earth and Other Poems*. New York: Random House, 1988.

Ugah, Ada. *Songs of Talakawa*. Devon: Merlin Books, 1983.

Zimunya, Musaemura. *Thought Tracks*. Burnt Mill: Longman, 1982.

7

Reclaiming the Initiative from the *Malestream:* Themes in African Women's Poetry

In written African literature, male poets are everywhere visible and female poets are barely seen, at times not seen. Female voices in modern African poetry have been highly marginalized. However, a close look at the heritage of African poetry shows that women poets were (and still are) as many, if not more than male poets in the oral traditional practice. Every aspect of the traditional African woman's life is marked by songs. Their songs include lullabies, work songs, praise songs, abuse songs, dirges, and chants to gods and goddesses.

In modern times, with writing women poets have either been culturally handicapped or ignored, which gives the impression that the written poetry is only, if not mainly, a male preserve. As Frank Chipasula puts it, "African women poets are engaged in a double struggle out of invisibility and silence under patriarchy, and they bear the double burden of colonial and male oppression. By insisting to unchain their voices and sing their songs, the women poets are challenging both the male tradition of written African poetry and reclaiming their historical role as the primal singers in African societies" (29).

The neglect of African female poets started, as Frank and Stella Chipasula rightly observe, from Léopold Sédar Senghor's *Anthologie de la Nouvelle Poésie Nègre et Malgache de la Langue Française* published in1948. This neglect or underestimation of women voices is continued in Gerald Moore and Ulli Beier's *Modern Poetry from Africa* (1963), which for a long time was the classic anthology of modern African poetry. Only two women, the Mozambican Noemia de Sousa and the São Toméan Alda do Espirito Santo (presented by the editors as male) were entered, despite some well-known women poets such as Gladys Casely-Hayford and Mabel Segun. In the Moore-Beier revision of the anthology into the *Penguin Book of Modern African Poetry* (1982), only Molara Ogundipe-Leslie was added. Isidore Okpewho's *Heritage of African Poetry* (1985) totally excludes modern African women poets.

The Heinemann Book of African Poetry in English (1990) has some three women: Marjorie Oludhe Macgoye of Kenya and both Molara Ogundipe-Leslie and Catherine Acholonu of Nigeria. *The Fate of Vultures: New Poetry of Africa* (1989), a BBC poetry competition selection, features a few women poets. *Voices from the Fringe* (1988), an anthology of young Nigerian poets, has many female poets, though still generally under-represented.

It is in light of this lack of a comprehensive book on African women poets that the recent *Heinemann Book of African Women's Poetry* (1995) edited and introduced by Stella and Frank M. Chipasula is an epoch-breaking publication. Here at last is a work bringing together the poetic harvest of African women poets from the Egyptian woman Pharaoh Hatshepsut through women poets involved in the colonial struggle such as Anna Greki of Algeria and Noemia de Sousa of Mozambique to such a young poet as Kristina Rungano of Zimbabwe born in 1963. Also in 1995 Malthouse Press of Lagos published *New Poets of West Africa*, an anthology edited by the Gambian writer Tijan Sallah. This fresh anthology includes, among others, Molara Ogundipe-Leslie, Catherine Acholonu, Phanuel Egejuru, Abena Busia, and Irene Assiba d'Almeida.

Published poetry works of individual female poets are few and this situation could worsen under weak economic conditions and flagging interest in education in Africa and the demotion of poetry at the expense of fiction and drama in Europe and North America. The few women poets are published by very small presses as is the case with Ifi Amadiume, Micere Mugo, and Zindzi Mandela (*Black as I am*). Catherine Acholonu's works are published privately and have not been widely distributed. Thus works of African female poets do not appear to be well exposed to generate critical interest. However, now there are many anthologies of their poetry out there for any interested critic to have enough material for a serious study.

Pre-Literate Oral/Traditional Poetry

Traditionally, African women held the initiative over men in poetry which is sung or chanted. After all,

> African women have been historically custodians and repositories of cultural as well as spiritual values which they have embodied in their pounding songs, millet-threshing songs, harvesting songs, songs that affirm values and heighten the sense of community. Women simultaneously utilize these songs as a means of censoring anti-social behaviour, critiquing sexual inequality, and protesting against male oppression. Accompanying their work with song, our mothers trans-

form drudgery into rhythmic and dance patterns that neutralize its potentially adverse effects on the human body and psyche (Chipasula 4).

Themes of such songs include containing loneliness after separation from a lover, love, lamenting barrenness, gratitude to her god(dess) for giving her a child, and in polygamous households expressing bad feelings towards a husband or rival. Interestingly, some of these themes are still pursued by modern African women poets. In West Africa there were (and still are) griots and griottes. Even in the area of the epic which has been presented as always a male preserve, there are women epic singers. I have personally researched on a female of the Yungur people of northeastern Nigeria whose epic "Kwa lau" is remarkable for its powerful images and unique female heroic voice. Themes of traditional women's poetry therefore also involve ethnic pride, the equivalent of modern nationalism.

Colonialism and Writing

Men generally had a headstart in Western education in Africa, hence there are many male writers. Most parents appeared to have been overprotective of their daughters and so did not send them to school in large groves, unlike boys they encouraged to go to school so as to know the European ways. There is no doubt that there is a symbiotic relationship between Western education and creative writing in modern Africa. Also colonialism, an arm of imperialism, was seen more as a male thing as the colonial administrators were white males whose wives occasionally visited but were more seen than heard.

African culture has not helped women to be free, adventurous, and expressive publicly as modern poetry desires. It is not that women did not and do not sing lewd songs in traditional society, but such performance was collective rather than individualistic. Today women writers appear more visible as fiction writers and dramatists than poets. It seems that the stature and number of African women in fiction surpass those in modern poetry. The culture does not seem to promote private experiences of women to be broadcast in print. In other words, women are inhibited culturally to write about their private experiences. I have talked to several women who hide their poems from their husbands because they feel should their private feelings be known, their marriages would be in trouble. There are many married male poets with love poems not written for their wives who do not feel any qualms being published. I am yet to read an African female poet who is married writing a love poem to another man who is not a blood relation.

In any case, the cultural situation of women with the paucity of their published poetic output has led to the appropriation of the human voice by men, but this is not complete and only an inclusive consciousness can reveal Africa's true nature. Also there is the need for complementarity of the genders for strength in Africa, where women who appear to form a majority are often underestimated or ignored in their creative output.

Historical Themes of African Women

African women poets have from the beginning of writing in the continent ranged with their male counterparts in struggling against foreign aggression, colonialism, and racism. The Portuguese brutal colonization of São Tomé and Mozambique, the French colonization of Algeria, and the white minority domination of South Africa through apartheid are some of the main cases in which African women poets were in the forefront of nationalist struggle.

The Mozambican Noemia de Sousa blazed the poetic trail for African women writers in her socio-political consciousness. Such a committed poet, her protest poems "helped fan the fire of anti-colonial resistance among intellectuals. In her poems she, like her male counterparts, protested not only against contract or forced labor, oppression, injustice, and forced cultivation of such cash crops as cotton or cashew nuts but also the export of migrant labor to the South African gold and diamond mines as well as the deportation of laborers to the coffee and cocoa plantations of São Tomé" (Chipasula 7). In her "If You Want to Know Me," she invites the outsider to know the African through the folk art, a black wooden Makonde sculpture, which symbolizes the dignity of the African. Apart from the Negritude theme of extolling the beauty of blackness, she also expresses the unifying role of art in a multi-ethnic state. She wants those who want to know her to

> examine with careful eyes
> this bit of black wood
> which some unknown Makonde brother
> cut and carved
> with his inspired hands
> in the distant lands of the North   (Chipasula 121).

De Sousa identifies with African-American singers (Paul Robeson and Marian) she has not met but are from "the same blood and of the same beloved sap of Mozambique." She adds: "I shall not be distracted by the light music / of Strauss's waltzes." In "Call" she protests against both male and colonial oppression. In the poem she recalls a "sister,"

"One child on her back, another in her belly / — ever and ever again!" tortured to death in the cause of her struggle (Stella and Frank Chipasula 164). There is the double entendre in "Our Voice" as de Sousa protests against "the white selfishness of men" (idem 165). There is the strong suggestion of whites and men being *her* oppressors. As Chipasula puts it, "the disadvantages of gender, race and class constitute a triple yoke that grips the Mozambican peasant woman. Sexually exploited by her own man, she has simultaneously been lashed by the 'mean and brutal rhino-whip' of the colonial administrator" (13).

Another well-known lusophone African female poet is Alda do Espirito Santo of the plantation island of São Tomé. She calls for the solidarity of all Africans suffering under colonialism in "The Same Side of the Canoe." "Grandma Mariana" paints a pathetic picture of what slavery can do to a woman—make her mad. After the massacre of African civilians in February 1953, she wrote "Where are the men chased away by this mad wind?" which earned her arrest. Her poetry supports the working class: washer women, dock workers, and plantation workers. Her poems "indicate that the major preoccupations of colonized African women poets do not differ from those of their male counterparts" (Chipasula 15). Women may suffer two or three-fold because of their gender and class, but Alda do Espirito Santo focuses on the need for solidarity of all the colonized people against their oppressors. She is in fact the predecessor of the African male writers of the 1980s who wrote in support of the disadvantaged and the working class.

The Theme of Combat: The Example of Algerian and South African Poets

The Algerian war for independence produced many female poets. The best known are Anna Greki, Daniele Amrane, and Malika O'Lahsen. These accomplished female poets turned "from purely anti-colonial poetry that listed colonial abuses to a poetry that validated the armed struggle as a legitimate way of achieving freedom in that country" (Chipasula 19). Leila Djabali's "For My Torturer, Lieutenant D..." records what the Algerian female suffered during the war. In the poem, she gives a detailed and passionate account of her torture:

> You slapped me—
> no one had ever slapped me—
> electric shock
> and then your fist
> and your filthy language
> I bled too much....

The torturer-soldiers were the same, "as alike as two drops of blood," in their sadism and inhumanity and the poet wonders whether they have mothers and wives.

South African women poets have also treated the theme of combat from different perspectives. Amelia Blossom Pegram reflects the South African reality in apartheid days in her criticism of the wielders of apartheid. In a sarcastic but pungent voice in "Burials," she says:

> those children of Dimbaza had no time
> to be bright and beautiful
> i have run out of hymns
> i cannot cry all day   (Stella and Frank Chipasula 188).

She condemns the division of society on color line and the killing and neglect of blacks. In "Deliverance," using the image of a pregnant woman in labour, she symbolically describes South Africa's struggle for freedom:

> Bear down
> My Mother Country
> Push
> You who have carried the seeds
> full term
> Bear down
> Push
> Only you can give birth
> to our freedom...   (Stella and Frank Chipasula 189).

In the same anti-apartheid perspective is Ingrid Jonker's "The Child who was Shot Dead by Soldiers at Nyanga" in which the poet laments the death of innocence as this child's case reflects a wide-ranging abuse of black children by white soldiers.

Diversity of Themes

Themes of modern/contemporary African women poets are so diverse and complex that they cannot be pigeon-holed. In many cases, they are the same as those expressed by male poets. They complement the male voices for the truly human and African. However, there are certain themes which are specifically expressed by women: those that deal with their oppression in the African patriarchy and themes which focus on their body. Even their expression of love differs from the male poets'. Micere Mugo's "I Want You to Know" is erotic in a particularly female way:

I want you to know
how carefully
I watered the tender shoots
you planted
in my little garden

(*Daughter of My People Sing*, Nairobi, 1976).

Most African women's love poems are not in the vein of Micere Mugo's "I Want You to Know" as there is a certain ambivalence in needing and enjoying love and yet finding it painful. Ifi Amadiume's "The Union" pursues this theme. Many African women poets are skeptical of love. Molara Ogundipe-Leslie's "Yoruba Love" is very sarcastic of the love African men have for their women. There is some distrust of love as something that benefits men at the expense of the women.

Mainstream/*Male*stream

Mabel Segun in both "The Smart One" and "Corruption" in *Conflict* deals with the social malaise of her Nigerian society. Hers is socio-political criticism as in most modern African poets of both the first and the second generations. The theme of exile with its accompanying loneliness and pain is dealt with by Abena Busia in *Testimonies of Exile*. Like the criticism of socio-political corruption, there is nothing particularly female in this theme which has been dealt with at one time or another by male poets like Dennis Brutus, Kofi Awoonor, and Frank Chipasula. Busia recollects past experiences in her home country of Ghana and finds christianity as a spiritual and psychological refuge.

Catherine Acholonu expresses the traditional theme of womanhood. She talks of responsible motherhood in "The Spring's Last Drop," where "I Obianuju / I shall provide my children / with plenty" (17). As I have stated in the preceding chapter,

Reinforcing her acceptance of the traditional role of responsible motherhood, "Lost Virtue" laments the emergence of the modern woman. She is strongly rooted in tradition which is manifested in her role as mother and priestess and her being anchored on her father and husband.

Feminist Themes

Ogundipe-Leslie in "On Reading an Archeological Article" strikes a different chord from the male poets:

They would say that she of the neck like a duiker's
Whose breasts are the hills of Egypt

Who weeps the Nile from her eyes of antimony
Is but another cosmopolitan housewife
Smart enough to walk ten paces behind her Mr. Doe.

O Akhnaton!

How long shall we speak to them
Of the difference without bane
How long shall we say another world lives
Not spinned on the axis of maleness
But rounded and wholed, charting through
Its many runnels its justice distributive?
O Nefertiti...   (Maja-Pearce 184).

This is a distinctly female voice. There is the use of "we" to identify
herself as female, a gender-specific identity absent in male poets. Here
"we" refers to women, while "them" refers to men. The dichotomy is
best illustrated in male exploitation, abuse, brutalization, oppression of
the female culturally, socially, and otherwise. The use of the apostrophe
highlights the passionate feeling and exasperation of the female speaker
of the poem. Ogundipe-Leslie's "Yoruba Love" also treats this theme.

The exploitation of women is a common theme in many African female poets. Mabel Segun's "Exploitation" deals with this male exploitation of women:

Ready to be plucked, she was,
Like a coconut;
The warm milk from her swollen breast
They drained without regard
For the emptiness they left behind.
I saw her plump and ripened flesh
Shredded and chewed into tiny bits.
I saw them use her—
Or what was left of her—
As a footmat;
And when that got worn
They threw it out
Onto the dung heap
and moved away
To greener pastures   (7).

In this poem, men are portrayed as eternal predators of women.
Women are seen as victims of male lust. In Acholonu's "Other forms of
slaughter," men are presented through images as beasts. This female
perception of men as violators of women cuts across religious and age

lines. Nana Aisatu Magajgi, a Muslim lady from Gombe in Nigeria, shows similar anger in "I see it all:"

> I see sister
> Battered by poverty
> And made to sell her wares
> In markets of condescension
>
> I see her
> Wielding mercenary smiles
> Skin bruised
> To please the lusty pack
>
> I see her
> Lured into brothels...
> ....
>
> Like a lame antelope
> She will fall to her hunters
> And all alone
> She will bear accursed scars   (Garuba 13).

The image of the hunter and the hunted is very significant to show the women as victims. Women are presented as victims that greedy men use to fill their desires and egos. Again Magaji's poem shows women as disadvantaged culturally, socially, and economically because of their gender.

In many African women poets, being a woman means suffering. Ama Ata Aidoo in "Issues" feels that women suffer daily in the process of going about to get the necessary things for meals, whereas men feel that providing money is enough. In Micere Mugo's "Wife of the Husband" the woman labors as the man snores. Women harbor such bitterness towards men that Ifi Amadiume in "Bitter" writes:

> If you were to squeeze me and wash,
> squeeze me and wash,
> squeeze me and wash,
> and I foam,
> again and again,
> like bitter-leaf
> left out too long to wither,
> you would not squeeze
> the bitterness out of me   (44).

To this female poet, male abuse is personal. She uses repetition to passionately emphasize her lasting bitterness against male abuse.

It is worthy of note that in the same female poet's work there could be poems which suggest opposition to women's liberation as in Mabel Segun's "Women Together," in which she ridicules women's solidarity and liberation and concludes that "Liberation begins at home" (22).

The African Woman's Body

Many African women poets deal with a broad theme that involves the woman's body, sex and sexuality, motherhood and labor. The British-born French-speaking Egyptian Joyce Mansour in "A Woman Kneeling in the Sorry Jelly" writes about menopause and the anxieties women feel about that phase of their lives. Irene Assiba d'Almeida describes the pangs of labor. Perhaps the most covered aspect of womanhood in African women's poetry is labor. Micere Mugo alludes to it in "Wife of the Husband." Jeni Couzyn treats it in "The Pain" as also do Amelia Pegram in "Deliverance," Lindiwe Mabuza in "Dream Cloud," Ingrid Jonker in "Pregnant Woman," and Kristina Rungano in "Labour." Labor is the most defining aspect of womanhood to these African poets. Images of pain, blood, and hurt characterize these poems on labor. Shakuntala Hawoldar focuses on the specific condition of being a woman and talks of her being "sleepless" with "sores inside" in "You Have Touched my Skin." Images of violation, penetration, and wounds copiously describe the woman's pain as a result of sex and consequent pregnancy and labor. Labor reflects not only their suffering and fertility but also their enduring ability to go through pain for the love of the newborn.

Mabel Tobrise, a young Nigerian poet, deals extensively in her manuscript titled *Poems Out of Hiding* with the theme of the woman's body. Even the title of the poetry manuscript itself shows a lack of inhibition uncommon in African women writers' works. In "My Body" she says "Me and my body are one whole, / and no hole" (3). Her poem "Clitoridectomy" tells what only the African woman who has gone through the experience can best express. Other poems such as "Preying" and "Matriarchy" satirize the African patriarchy that generally leaves the woman in a subordinate position. Tobrise reflects more the female spirit of the late 1980s and 1990s than most of the earlier female poets discussed.

Conclusion

African female poets no doubt add variety to modern African poetry. There are certain themes which are the same with those of male poets. There seems to be a clear pattern that where there has been a national political struggle with an external or racial aggressor as in Mozambique, São Tomé, Algeria, and South Africa, female voices tend to be the same as male voices. At periods of national emergencies, women see themselves as patriots and struggle jointly with men. Even when gender issues arise, they are not highlighted. But at other times, the female poets fight against patriarchal and other male forms of oppression.

A fairly young tradition, it seems the women poets tend to deal with more immediate themes first. Since African patriarchies seem to render women disadvantaged, marginalised, and bitter, protest against male oppression is common. With such images of oppression as the donkey, violation, and body bruises, the female poets passionately establish the female identity by using "we" to represent them as victims of men. This conflict between their vulnerability and the men's power is common in many of their poems. As the women speak about the woman's body, they help to establish a full African psyche, which has been hitherto misappropriated by male poets.

One might be tempted to ask, where are the Léopold Sédar Senghors, Christopher Okigbos, and Wole Soyinkas among the women poets? There are Noemia de Sousa and Alda do Espirito Santo. But even if in the overall poetic scene, women have not been as visible as men, there are reasons. Since men had a headstart in Western education, women are just catching up and as society becomes more liberal in the African patriarchies, they will have the time and space in their lives to write about more philosophical and metaphysical themes that some of the established male poets write on. An area one would expect women to dominate is love poetry, but with very few exceptions cultural and social inhibitions seem to limit their public expression. One would also want the women poets to reconnect with tradition so as to imbibe the qualities that made and still make traditional female oral artists great. Significantly, the women poets speak for themselves and do not need to be spoken for by male voices.

References and Works Cited

Anyidoho, Kofi and Peter Porter and Musaemura Zimunya. *The Fate of Vultures: New Poetry of Africa*. Oxford: Heinemann, 1989.

Amadiume, Ifi. *Passion Waves*. London: Karnak House, 1985.

Busia, Abena P. A. *Testimonies of Exile*. Trenton, New Jersey: AWP, 1990.

Chipasula, Frank M. *When My Brothers Come Home: Poems from Central and Southern Africa*. Middletown, CT: Wesleyan UP, 1985.

———. "Remembering Forgotten Singers: Re-Assembling Contemporary African Women Poets' Voices," unpublished essay.

————. with Stella Chipasula. eds. *The Heinemann Book of African Women's Poetry* Oxford, U.K: Heinemann, 1995.

Garuba, Harry. *Voices from the Fringe*. Lagos: Malthouse, 1988.

James, Adeola. *In Their Own Voices: African Women Writers Talk*. Oxford: Heinemann, 1990.

Maja-Pearse, Adewale. ed. *The Heinemann Book of African Poetry in English*. Oxford: Heinemann, 1990.

Mugo, Micere Githae. *Daughter of My People Sing*. Nairobi: East Africa Literature Bureau, 1976.

————. *My Mother's Poem and Other Songs*. Nairobi: East Africa Educational Publishers, 1994.

Ogundipe-Leslie, Molara. *Sew the Good Days*. Ibadan: Evans, 1985.

Sallah, Tijan. ed. *New Poets of West Africa*. Lagos: Malthouse, 1995.

Segun, Mabel. *Conflict and Other Poems*. Ibadan: New Horn, 1986.

Tobrise, Mabel I.E. *Poems Out of Hiding* (unpublished manuscript).

8

Branches of the Same Tree: African and African-American Poetry

Studies of African-American literary works often draw attention to the African cultural and racial origin. Residues of African culture no doubt exist in Black America and these apparently show in the creative expression. The indebtedness to African oral culture and folklore was a major feature of early African-American literature. The enslaved Africans in America had to adapt African tales and myths to their new environment. This influence extends through the Harlem Renaissance to contemporary African-American writings.

Henry Louis Gates sees the African trickster motif (the Yoruba variant in particular) mediated upon by the American environment in the works of Zora Neale Hurston, Ishmael Reed, and Alice Walker. John W. Roberts's *From Trickster to Badman: The Black Folk Hero in Slavery and Freedom* also treats the trickster motif, which originates from Africa. Joseph E. Holloway has edited a collection of essays under the title *Africanisms in American Culture*, some of which deal with folklore and other artistic expressions. These works which use African folkloric motifs to interpret African-American literature no doubt illuminate the works and deepen our understanding of the African-American literary tradition.

However, there seems to be other areas of comparison between African literature and African-American literature which go beyond cultural affinities per se. Even when culture is asserted, both modern Africans and African-Americans are using the same strategies to negate absorption into a foreign culture. There are thus common experiences arising from separate but related historical conditions, which bind American Blacks and Africans. Though Black America struggles against being absorbed into the Anglo-Saxon American mainstream in order to retain a black identity, it is neither African nor American mainstream. Thus African-American literature needs more than African culture and Western literary aesthetics to interpret it.

It is in this light that Sonia Sanchez's question "Are we not more than color and drums?" (84) is pertinent. Africans and African-Americans share experiences which transcend color. I therefore want to do a comparative study of modern African and African-American poetry with a view to showing similarities in the works as a result of conditions prevailing in Africa as well as in Black America. Such conditions include poverty, self-assertion, and identity.

I am aware of the "great cultural differences between literatures which are produced by a Black minority in a rich and powerful white country and those produced by the Black majority population of an independent nation" (Ashcroft, Griffiths and Tiffin 21). While "this is especially so since the latter nations are often still experiencing the residual effects of foreign domination in the political and economic spheres" (Ashcroft et al. 21), the institution of slavery has lasting effects on African-American consciousness. The post-independence status of Africa is comparable to the post-Emancipation of African-Americans.

American Blacks have at various times established alliances with African peoples for reasons other than of race. As Maulana Karenga puts it, "there are concrete bases for alliances among Third World peoples growing out of their situational similarity in that they are oppressed and exploited on the bases of race and class" (256). It is this "situational similarity" between Africans and African-Americans that I want to explore in African-American poetry. African-Americans may have a different geographical space—the US of America—but they share the same consciousness with Africans culturally, historically, and in other ways. As I have indicated earlier, African peoples see the current phase of their history as mainly post-independence, which is analogous to the post-1862 Emancipation Proclamation, or at best post-Civil Rights Act of 1964 for African-Americans.

It is not only that Sonia Sanchez was influenced by the Nigerian Christopher Okigbo as in her "elegy," not only that an Ethiopian-owned Africa World Press published *Under a Soprano Sky*, not only that the poets I am going to discuss are Black, but they all express an African consciousness in the American environment in their writings. Significantly, on the back of the front cover of Carolyn Rodgers's *Songs of a Black Bird*, published by Third World Press in Chicago (1969), there is a "statement of purpose" by the editors:

> The Third World is a liberating concept for people of color, non- europeans—for Black people. That world has an ethos a black aesthetic if u will—and it is the intent of Third World Press to capture that ethos, that black energy. We publish black...for Africans here...and Africans abroad.

Third World is used here to designate the conditions of Africa, not necessarily its race. However, the emphasis remains Africa and Africans.

I will discuss the poetry of Arna Bontemps, Sonia Sanchez, Carolyn Rodgers, and Audre Lorde as African-American works which express the same consciousness as in modern African poetry. The selection of these poets is based on the availability of their works despite the lack of adequate criticism of the works themselves. Many of the qualities I find in their works may also be found in many other African-American poets.

Blacks in the United States face problems that most Africans faced and still face. Their culture is being absorbed by white/Western culture. In elementary schools, high schools, and colleges, Black works are not taught, or at best taught from a Eurocentric perspective. For a long time images of Tarzan and other negative myths about the black person have made African-Americans to hate themselves for being black. They were alienated from their African culture, which was presented by the mainstream as primitive. Since the introduction of Black Studies programs in the late 1960s, some attempt has been made to recognize Black culture in the curriculum. The mainstream American culture is white Anglo-Saxon with its Hellenistic roots. Many sensitive Blacks have to decolonise their minds like colonized peoples do because they suffer from cultural alienation. The tension in Gabriel Okara's "Piano and Drums" is comparable to the "double consciousness" that W.E.B. Du Bois highlighted about American Blacks who are torn between remaining black or getting integrated. African-Americans, like the speaker of Okara's poem, are

> ...lost in the morning mist
> of an age at a riverside keep
> wandering in the mystic rhythm
> of jungle drums and the concerto   (20).

The same sentiments of conflict of cultures and the need to maintain an African identity is in Okot p'Bitek's *Song of Lawino*. For American Blacks who want to be their Black selves, resisting white culture leads to cultural assertiveness and liberation.

Since poets generally are cultural standard-bearers of their people, it is not surprising that cultural assertiveness is a predominant preoccupation in African-American poetry. Cultural assertiveness manifests itself in many ways in African-American poetry. In no periods has cultural nationalism been so important in African-American literature as in the Harlem Renaissance and the Civil Rights years of the late 1960s and the early 1970s. It is significant that all four poets being discussed belong to these literary movements: Arna Bontemps was a major figure of the Harlem Renaissance; Carolyn Rodgers, Sonia Sanchez, and Audre Lorde all lived through the Civil Rights movement period of Black Power. Both the Harlem Renaissance and the Black Power movement were protest periods in which African-Americans asserted their Black identity so as not to be absorbed into the white monolith.

Some of the works of the Harlem Renaissance period compare in their protest and cultural assertiveness with Negritude works. In Arna Bontemps's *Personals*, the poet identifies himself as a Black man who is different from the mainstream American. In "God Give To Men," there are the "yellow man," "blue-eyed men," and the "black man," whose "meed / of laughter, / his cup of tears" the poet wants God to "fill afresh" (11). The poet thus carves a unique identity for the Black person as opposed to other peoples. Bontemps concludes "The Return" with

> Darkness brings the jungle to our room:
> the throb of rain is the throb of muffled drums.
> Darkness hangs our room with pendulums
> of vine and in the gathering gloom
> our walls recede into a denseness of
> surrounding trees. This is a night of love
> retained from those lost nights our fathers slept
> in huts; this is a night that must not die.
> Let us keep the dance of rain our fathers kept
> and tread our dreams beneath the jungle sky   (12).

In this poem Bontemps passionately evokes images of traditional Africa from which the forebears of African-Americans were taken into slavery. Bontemps's call for a return to the ways of "our fathers" reminds one of Léopold Sédar Senghor's expression of similar emotions in, among others, "In Memoriam" and "Night of Sine." In both Bontemps and Senghor, there is an idyllic picture of Africa, which is generally romanticized. Bontemps's cultural assertiveness like that of his colleagues of the Harlem Renaissance such as Claude McKay and Langston Hughes must be understood in the light of racial discrimination in America which has continued a century after the Emancipation and decades after different Civil Rights Acts were enacted. In other words, as African people try to assert themselves culturally after colonialism, so do African-American people after regaining their freedom.

Carolyn Rodgers who lived through the Civil Rights/Black Power movement period in her 1975 poetry collection, *how i got ovah*, culturally asserts her Black heritage in "and when the revolution came:"

> . . . we got to
> build black institutions where our children
> call each other sister and brother
> and can grow beautiful, black and strong and grow in
>   black grace   (66).

The Black Power movement made Blacks to understand their culture and assert their African heritage. Also Audre Lorde, a primary link between Africa and Black America because of her immediate Caribbean ancestry, defines her Blackness in relation to Africa. In *Our Dead Behind Us*, she alludes to Yoruba and Fon myths of Western Nigeria and Dahomey (now Benin Republic) respectively. She defines her gender in terms of African history and folklore as she takes the Amazons, African women warriors of fame, as her ancestors and mentors. In *From a Land Where Other People Live*, Lorde treats the theme of cultural identity in both "Black Mother Woman" and "The Winds of Orisha" among others. While identity is a complex issue in Lorde because she is not only Black but also a woman and a lesbian, she continuously harps on her Caribbean and African roots, which give her an anchor in the American sea of cultures. In "Call," the poet invokes Aido Hwedo:

> I am a Black woman turning
> mouthing your name as a password
> through seductions self-slaughter
> and I believe in the holy ghost
> mother
> in your flames beyond our vision
> blown light through the fingers of women
> enduring warring   (*Our Dead Behind Us*, 74).

Invocation is a common feature of modern African poetry as shown in Okigbo's invocation of "Mother Idoto" in *Labyrinths*, Soyinka's invocation of Ogun in "O Roots!" (*A Shuttle in the Crypt*), and mine of Aridon in *The Fate of Vultures*. As African writers assert themselves culturally against colonialism, neocolonialism, and other assimilating tendencies, so do African-American writers do against being assimilated into the Anglo-Saxon white culture.

The history of African-Americans, apart from being interwoven in parts, compares in many ways with that of Africans. As African literature, for instance, reflects African history, so does African-American literature reflect Black history. Slavery is the ultimate form of domination. The Emancipation Proclamation of 1862 is like the political independence of African countries that were once colonized. As African-Americans have continued to fight for their rights as free citizens, so do most Africans fight for freedom and rights even after political independence in their own countries. It is understandable why African-Americans have had coalitions with African peoples, supported independence movements and demonstrated an anti-colonial perspective. As an oppressed people who are discriminated against, African-Americans have used poetry as a weapon to fight for freedom. What Evangelista says of Third World literature is true of both African and African-American literatures in being "history-based,...often political and it *does* carry a call to action" (6).

There is no doubt that much of African-American poetry is political. All four poets under discussion are political in their expression of the historical experience of Black Americans. Arna Bontemps in "A black man talks of reaping" expresses the hard labor heritage of Blacks and their exploitation from the days of slavery. Though the poet uses a personal voice, he is expressing the general Black experience when he says that "my heart has known its winters and carried gall" (26). Here the poet is talking symbolically of the harsh Black experience in America from slavery to the poet's time. Similarly, Carolyn Rodgers expresses the African-American historical experience in "Non-Poem," one of the poems in *Songs of a Black Bird*. The poet exhorts fellow Blacks to "keep on pushin." It is significant that the collection is dedicated to Love, Truth, Organization, Discipline, and Liberation.

In fact, the Black Art movement of the 1960s influenced both Rodgers and Sanchez, some of whose poems express protest and Black nationalism in the manner of African literature in colonial and post-independence times. Sanchez's "Letter to Dr. Martin Luther King" in *homegirls & handgrenades* is history-based. Sanchez from the beginning has been a political poet. In *Home Coming*, "for unborn malcolms" expresses her radical politics:

> git the word out
> now.
> to the man/boy
> taking a holiday
> from murder.
>   tell him
> we hip to his shit and that
> the next time he kills one
> of our
>   blk/princes
>   some of his faggots
> gonna die
>   a stone/cold/death.
>   yeah.
> It's time.
>   an eye for an eye
>   a tooth for a tooth
>   don't worry bout his balls
> they al
>   ready gone.

                    git the word
        out that us blk/niggers
                    are out to lunch
        and the main course
        is gonna be his white meat.
                    yeah   (28).

While the assassination of Malcolm X was its immediate inspiration,
this poem carries the entire history of the hostile relationship between
whites and blacks in America. There is a black/white conflict and the
exploited Blacks are passionately calling for retaliation.

The Black/White situation in the United States is in many ways comparable to similar conflict situations in Africa. In Africa, the conflict
once arose out of the colonial experience, which though out in most
places has been replaced by the neo-colonial factor. Then there has been
the conflict between the haves and the have-nots, a euphemism for the
political elite and the impoverished masses. And there has been the in-
tractable conflict of apartheid in which Africans who live in their own
land have no basic political rights.

One of the defining features of Africa today is poverty. There is economic and political exploitation on both local and international levels.
Basic needs like food, health facilities, and education are not assured.
The majority of African people lack basic needs. Many African poets
including Lenrie Peters, Jared Angira, Syl Cheney-Coker, and Niyi Osundare have expressed concern with the socio-economic plight of the
common people of Africa. Cheney-Coker's "Peasants" and Angira's
"Quiet oratorio" are strong indictments of the exploiting ruling class
in Africa. Poverty is thus a major concern of African poets who generally range on the side of the economically disadvantaged masses.

In the United States, the ghettoization of Blacks is a Third World phenomenon in the so-called First World. According to Karenga, the ghetto
"not only closes Blacks in the community, but simultaneously shuts them
out from the access and various opportunities available in the larger society" (199). With the "general state of political and economic subordi-
nation...obvious and unarguable," Black Americans suffer from many
of the problems of under-developed peoples as in Africa. Poor Blacks are
hungry, without health insurance, and many are homeless.

African-American poets, mindful of their economic background,
write on the poverty of their people. Rodgers reflects Black poverty in
her family experience. In the third section of "For Our Father" in *how i
got ovah*, she writes:

    I had a puppy, and because we had rats in our home
    my mother laid poisoning on our bare dirt-part

> linoleum floors. And my puppy, being animal, being curious,
>   being stupid, ate the poison and died.
> Was the poison really for the rat, was it for the dog, or
> was it
>   for us...the Black niggers caught in the dirty
>   misery constrained ghetto?   (60).

Rodgers's experience is analogous to Arna Bontemps's "bitter fruit"(36). In subject matter, Rodgers's preoccupation is not different from what many African poets write about, as in Cheney-Coker's "Peasants" with

> the agony of imagining their squalor but never knowing it
> the agony of cramping them in roach infected shacks   (27).

The rat-infested house in Rodgers's poetry is a manifestation of the abject poverty in Black segments of the American society. African-American poets like Rodgers and Bontemps intuitively reflect an experience which Africans also know firsthand.

As a result of the shared experience of history, there is the expression of solidarity and kinship with others who suffer a similar plight of oppression and deprivation. This solidarity is on two levels: internal and external. African-Americans express a strong sense of kinship in their common culture and history and also express solidarity with others outside the United States, especially Africans. Sonia Sanchez's "Africa Poem No. 4" in *Under a Soprano Sky* expresses solidarity with Africa despite the continent's problems. She exhorts:

> ...Together. We
> will string our seeds
> . like viruses   (90).

It is because of this shared experience and sense of solidarity that the Kenyan writer Ngugi wa Thiongo says of Sonia Sanchez:

> In her writings I feel at home!
> In her house I feel at home!
> In her presence I feel at home!
>   (back cover of *Under a Soprano Sky)*.

Audre Lorde also expresses solidarity and kinship with people of Africa and of the Caribbean of African descent. Some of her poems talk of the situation in South Africa. In African-American poetry there is a plea for unity and solidarity to fight to eliminate the injustice against minority groups in America and other oppressed peoples of the world as in Africa. African-American literature is history-based as is their experience as a group. The odyssey from slavery through Emancipation and the Civil Rights movement to the continuing struggle against racism and discrimination is reflected in the poetry.

In the activist role of the African-American poet, he/she becomes a preacher and teacher to instill confidence and faith in themselves. Unlike mainstream American poetry which generally could pass for art for art's sake, African-American poetry is utilitarian and didactic like modern African poetry. There is a call for the human spirit to overcome all difficulties. Reading through most African-American poets of the 1920s, 1930s, 1960s and 1970s of the Harlem Renaissance and the Black Power/Black Art movements is like reading a war cry for cultural, social, and political unity. Claude McKay's "If We Must Die" and Amiri Baraka's "Black Art" are exhortations to Black people in America to resist being victimized by taking actions towards that effect. In "Masks" Sanchez appeals to African-Americans and Africans:

> o my people
> wear the white masks
> for they speak without speaking
> and hear words of forgetfulness.
> o my people   (48).

The title of this poem, "Masks," is itself a symbol of an African identity. This poem treats the same theme with Senghor's poem of the same title. Thus, like African literature, African-American poetry is more community and people-oriented. The poets are like priests and teachers of their people, whom they appeal to for a change in consciousness to act for their group survival.

A common feature of African literature is the moral uprightness of the people in contrast to the immorality and a-morality of their colonial exploiters and later of the indigenous ruling class. Negritude writers like Léopold Senghor and David Diop have explored this theme in many of their poems. The "native values" are generally presented as superior to the debauched imperialist ones. Okot p'Bitek does this in his *Song of Lawino*. The spirituality and world-view of the "natives" are contrasted with the materialism of the imperialists.

In the United States, the whites who enslaved Africans are the immoral group because of the sadistic and exploitative nature of slavery. The whites therefore carry the guilt of imperialists. African-Americans are quick to remind whites of the travesty of slavery. Bontemps reflects the African-American moral outrage of a spiritual people against an oppressive godless group. "Southern Mansion" deals with the contrast between the white slave-master and the tortured slave:

> There is a sound of music echoing
> through the open door
> and in the field there is
> another sound tinkling in the cotton:
> chains of bondmen dragging on the ground   (16).

Audre Lorde's "Equal Opportunity" is satiric of the American system represented by the deputy assistant secretary of defense and American troops in Grenada. Lorde criticizes the militaristic ruling elite in Washington as many African poets satirize their governments. Writing on a Grenadan girl whose father was killed, Lorde exposes the contradiction of America's liberating role. Despite the long history of African-Americans in the United States, they have not come to see themselves as mainstream; they are the "other" group that has been immorally treated as slaves and are still being discriminated against, oppressed, exploited, and marginalized.

A further aspect of Africanity in African-American poetry shows in the style and use of language. As indigenous languages inform English in Achebe and Soyinka, so does the African-American variety of English with its Africanisms inform the poetic language. In addition, many African poets use pidgin English, which is a blend of African language patterns and English. Mainstream English is as much a second language in the Black community as it is in Africa. Many African-Americans upon going to school have to learn "good English." The Black dialect has its own prosody and semantic register. The popular terms such as "bad" and "dead" show how the standard American English can be turned around by African-Americans. The attempt to use a folk style to reach as many people as possible and also to reflect the Black experience as a people compares with modern African literary aims. Also as the English language is being revitalized by its non-native writers of Africa such as Achebe and Soyinka, so does the African-American idiom impact upon English to result in a new freshness and vigor.

The title of Carolyn Rodgers's collection, *how i got ovah*, is a pointer to the use African-American writers make of English. The use of the Black variety of English affords the poet wider nuances, wit, and humor on many occasions. Sonia Sanchez's "haiku" in *Under a Soprano Sky* combines wit and humor:

> i works hard but treated
> bad man. i'se telling you de
> truth i full of it   (52).

Her *We A BaddDDD People* uses Black slang which not only makes the poetry accessible to most African-American folks who share her experience but also identify her unconventional attitude in the American society. She uses "BaddDDD" to mean "nice" and "good." On a different level, Audre Lorde uses English modelled on African language patterns. For instance, the incantatory "Call" ends with lines that carry African ritual language patterns:

> I may be a weed in the garden
> of women I have loved
> who are still
> trapped in their season
> but even they shriek
> as they rip burning gold from their skins
> Aido Hwedo is coming
>
> We are learning by heart
> what has never been taught
> you are my given fire-tongued
> Oya Seboulisa Mawu Afrekete
> and now we are mourning our sisters
> lost to the false hush of sorrow
> to hardness and hatchets and childbirth
> and we are shouting
> Rosa Parks and Fannie Lou Hamer
> Assata Shakur and Yaa Asantewa
> my mother and Winnie Mandela are singing
> in my throat
> the holy ghosts' linguist
> one iron silence broken
> Aido Hwedo is calling
> calling
> your daughters are named
> and conceiving
> Mother loosen my tongue
> or adorn me
> with a lighter burden
>
> Aido Hwedo is coming.
>
> Aido Hwedo is coming.
>
> Aido Hwedo is coming   (74–75).

In the poem, Lorde brings together African and African-American women figures to underline their common origin and aspirations.

In conclusion, African-American poetry as exemplified by Arna Bontemps, Sonia Sanchez, Carolyn Rodgers, and Audre Lorde shares common thematic and stylistic qualities with modern African poetry. The poetry is based on history, politics, and, above all, on the Black experience as a disadvantaged people in America. In their poverty and weak political position, they struggle to assert themselves culturally. From the experience of slavery, racism, and discrimination, the poets protest against their mistreatment. This makes the poetry generally radical in nature. The use of Black English by some of the poets establishes their literature as distinct from the mainstream. These experiential, historical, and linguistic aspects of African-American poetry are comparable to those of African poetry. This is in addition to having the same racial origin. These African and Afrocentric qualities of African-American poetry seem to have been strongest during the Harlem Renaissance represented by Bontemps and the years of the Civil Rights/Black Power/Black Art movement represented by Sanchez, Rodgers, and Lorde.

References and Works Cited

Angira, Jared. *Cascades*. London: Longman, 1979.

Ashcroft, Bill with Gareth Griffiths and Helen Tiffin. *The Empire Writes Back: Theory and Practice in Post-colonial Literatures*. London/New York: Routledge, 1989.

Bontemps, Arna. *Personals*. London: Paul Breman, 1973.

Cheney-Coker, Syl. *The Graveyard Also Has Teeth with Concerto for an Exile*. London: Heinemann, 1980.

Du Bois, W.E.B. *The Souls of Black Folk*. New York: Penguin, 1969.

Evangelista, Susan. "Third World Literature in the First World." Lecture in the English Department Lecture Series, University of Maiduguri (Nigeria), April, 1989.

Gates, Jr., Henry Louis. *The Signifying Monkey*. New York/Oxford: OUP, 1988.

Holloway, Joseph E. ed. *Africanisms in American Culture*. Bloomington: Indiana UP, 191.

Karenga, Maulana. *Introduction To Black Studies*. Los Angeles: U of Sankore Press, 1989.

Lewis, David. *When Harlem Was In Vogue*. New York/Oxford: OUP, 1979.

Lorde, Audre. *From a Land Where Other People Live*. Detroit: Broadside Press, 1973.

————. *Our Dead Behind Us*. New York: Norton, 1986.

Okara, Gabriel. *The Fisherman's Invocation*. Benin: Ethiope Press, 1979.

p'Bitek, Okot. *Song of Lawino*. Nairobi: EAPH, 1966.

Randall, Dudley. ed. *Black Poets*. New York: Bantam, 1971.

Roberts, John W. *From Trickster To Badman*. Philadelphia: U of Pennsylvania Press, 1990.

Rodgers, Carolyn. *Songs of a Black Bird*. Chicago: Third World Press, 1969.

———. *how i got ovah: new and selected poems*. Garden City, NJ: Anchor, 1975.

Sanchez, Sonia. *homegirls and handgrenades*. New York: Thunder's Mouth Press, 1984.

———. *Under a Soprano Sky*. Trenton, NJ: Africa World Press, 1987.

9

I Want to Be an Oracle:
My Poetry and My Generation

I was born at the right time. Though my mother was pregnant with me when the lunar eclipse of 1947 occurred, I did not arrive until April 24, 1948. I was born into an age of innocence in a rural home in the Delta region of Nigeria. The old ways were still very vibrant. I followed my grandparents to clear the thickly forested land for a farm and to plant yams. I followed my father and uncles to the palm-oil press, where palm seeds were prepared in a canoe-like wooden structure to produce palm oil. I participated in the village "undressing" of ponds, a full day's activity. I fished with hooks and caught big mudfish, which earned me my grandmother's praise. I followed my grandfather to set up his cone nets, I went on all-night fishing trips, I tapped rubber trees and earned money that made life comfortable all my youth.

While much of this period was an age of innocence, new ways were gradually creeping in and eroding some of the virtues of the old ones we cherished. Side by side, we practiced traditional dancing and gyrated to modern music. I watched masquerades in the village square during the Christmas season. At night we would have a social gathering, a euphemism for dancing with girls in the Western way. But compared to today, even those new ways were mild, harmless and interestingly innocent. Maybe an innocent people respond in a naive way to everything before them. I went to a Catholic school, was baptized and later confirmed in the Roman Catholic Church, but returned to serve as a priest or acolyte at the native shrine. Every first-born male in Urhobo is traditionally a priest. In fact, any male can be called upon at any time to act as priest. I saw my grandfather do so, and likewise my father and uncles. I myself was called upon at a very early age to perform the duties of a priest. I lived in two worlds simultaneously and did not feel torn apart as many others might have felt. I absorbed both ways well, since I saw school time as school time and time at home as time at home.

I think my poetry began from those days of going to school and learning to tell stories and going home to listen to my grandmother sing songs and tell folktales, myths, and legends of the Urhobo people. I always think of the tailor-ants' labyrinths, which are made of different types of leaves within their reach. This image eventually found its way into my early poetry in both *Children of Iroko & Other Poems* (1973) and

Labyrinths of the Delta (1986). Indigenous to the village of *iroko* trees, Okurunoh, the idyllic environment was imprinted in my early writing.

My roots thus run deep into the Delta area. Its traditions, folklore, fauna and flora no doubt enriched my *Children of Iroko* and *Labyrinths of the Delta*. This area of constant rains, where we children thought we saw fish fall from the sky in hurricanes, did not remain the same. By the 1960s the rivers had been dredged to take in pontoons or even ships to enter our backyard. Shell-BP had started to pollute the rivers, streams, and farmlands with oil and flaring gas. Forests had been cleared by poachers and others to feed the African Timber and Plywood Company in Sapele. Streams and marshes dried up. Rubber trees were planted in a frenzy to make money and were soon tapped to death. The *oware* fish that used to jump across culverts/roads were gone. There were no more fish in most of our waters. The heat from the blowout in Kokori and such places imperiled our lives and our means of sustenance. How quickly times had changed!

Memory is very important to the poet. Among my Urhobo people, poets and singers worship *Aridon,* god of memory, and *Uhaghwa,* god of inspiration and charming performance. Aridon is represented by a thread, which is meant to take one back to the source of past experiences. To me as a poet, childhood is vital, because it is the repository of memory. That is why the Delta area has been so important to me. I had quite an extraordinary youth, which still bubbles in my memory and writing. Those who grew up with me, of the same age or slightly older, used to say that I smiled a lot. My Delta years have become the touchstone with which I measure the rest of my life. The streams, the fauna, and the flora are the symbols I continually tap. Even when I wander outside to the many places I have experienced, that land of streams, the iroko tree, antelopes, anthills and so much life remains indelible in my memory and imprinted in my thought. Home remains for me the Delta, where I continue to anchor myself.

The world into which I was born has changed drastically over the years. It has gone without being replenished. We were partly responsible. We had no conservation policies strictly enforced. Though there were specific seasons for cutting palm-nut bunches, there were loopholes in other areas. As soon as Gamalin 20 came, people used it to wipe out the fish population. Forests were being denuded because my people did not believe in planting trees; that was an act of madness, according to them. My Grandmother told me of how Onoharigho, who first planted rubber trees, continued to be ridiculed until he became the richest man in the area!

But the major problem had to do with the discovery of oil in the Delta. The oil boom became doom for inhabitants of the region. The tension between what I knew as a child and what obtains now appears in my writing. My *Daydream of Ants* addresses the impact of modern (Western) technology on traditional African life and environment. "No Longer Our Own Country," in *The Blood of Peace* (1991), also addresses this senseless destruction of our original neighbors, the trees and animals.

> Our sacred trees have been cut down
> to make armchairs for the rich and titled;
> our totem eagle, that bird of great heights,
> has been shot at by thoughtless guardians...
> ....
> Where are the tall trees
> that shielded us from the sun's spears,
> where are they now that hot winds
> blow parching sands
> and bury us in dunes?

Images are bound to change. The tone of the poems also changes from the celebration of my childhood days to the anger of the 1970s and 1980s. This shift from a celebration of the environment to a lamentation for its demise reflects the reality of my experience. We have gradually been stripped and exposed to the elements.

Whether the poet was in me from birth or not, I was inspired to write by poets I read from an early age. Through my grandmother I had known traditional songs, and village life was filled with folklore and songs. By the time I went to school, and especially in my undergraduate years, I was exposed to a generation of African poets who had established strong voices: Léopold Senghor, Christopher Okigbo, Wole Soyinka, and J.P. Clark. There were also the Americans and British: Ezra Pound, whom I loved despite his sometimes fascist ideas; W.B. Yeats, whose use of Irish folklore drew him closer to me; and T.S. Eliot, who was impressive but inimitable. By the time I started to write, poetry was recognized as an intellectual art that most students feared and avoided. I loved it but wanted to carry it to the street and be different. At the time I attended Dan Izevbaye's class and ran a creative writers' club with Niyi Osundare, we were fortunate to have mentors in the persons of Okigbo, Soyinka, and Clark.

My relationship to these mentors was ambivalent. I liked them but would not wish to write like them. There was something in each that was extremely attractive. Okigbo so musical and free, Soyinka so concise and strong, Clark so sensuous and solid. At the same time, there was something in each that I wanted to avoid: Okigbo's obscurity, Soyinka's density, and Clark's occasional imitativeness. My professor saw me as a defender of Okigbo, but I might have grown to graft from each into my labyrinth only what would strengthen my craft. I shared with Clark the same cultural and physical background of the Delta, and I have always been compared to him. At the same time, I have used the verbal techniques of Soyinka and have always retained the musicality and incantatory rhythm of Okigbo. We cannot be like our masters and be ourselves. I started with these masters, whose style I admired in some ways and resisted in others. Perhaps this tension helped me to grow and become myself.

It was in the area of cultural exposition that those of my generation were to differ drastically from our predecessors. It was valid in their time to expose African culture after its denigration by colonialists in order to justify its blatant exploitation and racism. By my youth, culture had become basic and ordinary, like breathing. It was something we lived and did not need to display for others. Rather, socio-economic issues have become important. There had been an increasing erosion of the well-being I knew as a child. Time was that my mother would literally put a pot on the fire and then go and catch crayfish for palm-oil soup. Times have become very austere, ranging from such inconveniences as queuing to buy rice to severe shortages of basic needs. Hard times demand different attention than was the case in the "boom years."

I grew up in a period not of self-praise but of self-criticism. We have now come to hold our political leaders responsible for the deterioration of our well-being. Unlike the earlier generation that traced our problems to the colonial masters in London, Paris, Lisbon, and other places outside, we blame our brethren. Why are we so cursed, after being so blessed? The bogeyman in my time has not been an outsider but rather our own brother. It has become inadmissible to blame colonialism and the West for all of our current problems. We have replaced corrupt political leaders repeatedly with even more corrupt military leaders. As I have put it in "The African Nightmare," "It is not yet dawn, / and we wake from one nightmare / to another." How could we blame others for the Nigerian-Biafran war? Outsiders might have fueled the fire but we set it to burn ourselves. A teenager then in Warri, I witnessed both first the Biafran Army and then the Nigerian Army unleash savagery on people who were not of their ethnic groups. Soldiers on both sides killed for purely selfish ethnic reasons and never for national interests, as proclaimed. In the 1980s I visited the National War Museum and "Ojukwu's Bunker," both at Umuahia, and wrote "All that remains." The way innocent Igbo and Hausa people were hounded to death in Warri has affected my subsequent attitude toward life and society. It is with this background that I wrote "War Games:"

If your rivers swelled with cadavers,
if your college was the camp where
barbarians gambolled on corpses of other tribes,
if you saw officers on the loose in streets
all tainted dark red to the toe,
if you saw through masks of liberators
to thieving armies bolstering faith in blood relations

you would pull down Heroes' Arcade
and sleep over Remembrance Day.

My generation has not been given any latitude as to what it may write on. The age itself has conditioned our responses to it. We must attack with our pens one of two demons: corrupt civilian and military dictators. Literature might be devoted to leisure in other cultures, but for us Africans who are experiencing the second half of the twentieth century, literature must serve a purpose: to expose, embarrass, and fight corruption and authoritarianism. Literature has to draw attention to the increasing gap between the haves and the have-nots. Literature has become a weapon against the denial of basic human rights. In the 1960s and 1970s the focus was on political corruption, which was destroying the very fabric of good governance. In the 1980s and now socio-economic concerns have become dominant. Housing, food, health, and other basic needs which were taken for granted in the 1950s and early 1960s have become the focus of attention. It is understandable why the African artist is utilitarian. We do not have the luxury of some Western writers, who are apolitical and can afford to write art for art's sake and be confessional (a euphemism for self-therapy).

I believe in the artist's activist role. Action counts to remedy a bad situation. Being passive or apolitical will not change things. Patience may be a virtue in good times, but not in the desperate era in which Africans are living. Conditions unique to the Africa of my day have made me believe strongly that bad conditions do not change unless there is a persistent effort to reverse the current of evil. To accept the corruption as endemic and so insurmountable is to accept defeat. To accept the military's trampling of justice and freedom without protest or resistance is to accept a cursed life and to shirk one's responsibility. Not to act means hopelessness. I have hope. We are hopeful. However indirect we may have to be in our struggle, we are contributing to a dismantling of oppression and corruption. I have used the image of the struggle which collectively will destroy the oppressor.

The harassment of African writers by their governments has its roots in traditional culture. Spells were once cast on poets for satirizing and lampooning those who broke the social ethos and moral codes that governed the community. In the place of the traditional witch or wizard, there now stands the modern president, civilian or military. The situation is the same at one time or another in Ghana, Nigeria, Kenya, South Africa, and Malawi, among others. Instead of evil medicines in traditional times, there are now prisons and secret executions. This atmosphere of persecution has made the African literary artist in both traditional and modern times to operate under conditions of self-censorship. By the time I wrote "The Fate of Vultures" and "Players," I was aware that I could be jailed by the hyena in power. I bore no charm against oppression, much less tyranny. I had to use names which, though fictional, resonated with the actual names of the political and military leaders who were the subjects of my attacks. Everyone familiar with the Nigerian political scene of the early 1980s knows who Shamgari is. The same is true of "Alexius, architect of wind-razed mansions," and of the "player" who flashes his "toothsome pearls."

This self-censorship has stretched the imagination of many African poets. Fresh images and symbols have resulted from the search for a diction that would be an effective weapon against violators of the political ethos and at the same time a shield against persecution and libel for the writer. I have to call on images and characters from folklore in order to depict the contemporary situation. I have often resorted to the images of Eseze of the Okpe people, and Ogiso, a legendary tyrant of ancient Benin. Eseze was so tyrannical that his people plotted to have him killed in a most painful way: they dug a pit, rolled a mat over it, and placed a stool for him to sit on; he was chanted into his doom with the help of one of his wives, and as soon as he fell into the pit, the people poured boiling palm oil into the pit. In Ujevwe a king was buried with the paraphernalia of kingship. Ogiso in Urhobo legends sacrificed his people, many of whom had to flee the kingdom. There were leaders who asked their subjects who offended them to hold back a falling tree, which crushed them. As I imply in my poems, many of these legendary tyrants return to torment us. Symbolic animals and plants often appear to me to represent the current actors in the African scene. The poetry may be political as I attempt to reflect the condition of my people, but the language has to mediate between my call for the end of tyranny, corruption, and exploitation and the unique pleasure which poetry should also provide.

I do not consider myself unique in this endeavor, for my colleagues in Nigeria, Ghana, Malawi, Kenya, and elsewhere do likewise. The contemporary African writer has become a warrior of sorts, ever devising new strategies to deflect bullets from himself and still knock down the enemy. The logistics about which Okigbo talks in *Heavensgate* have become most relevant in our day. Poetry, indeed all African literature, has become the guidebook for achieving certain goals to benefit the common people. The poet has become primarily an activist.

Africa may be said to be the origin of humankind. It is naturally central to the whole world. However, it has been politically so marginalized that despite the fact that the equator divides it horizontally and the Greenwich line or prime meridian splits it vertically, Africa has long been contested by outsiders. In my time the Cold War was at its nastiest. In grammar-school days, I acted Lumumba's daughter in *Lumumba* and knew at an early age that some foreign agents, with the help of African hands such as Moise Tsombe and Mobutu, killed my hero. The Cold War forced Africa to identify with either the West or the East despite its so-called non-aligned status. We were again pawns in the larger world game being played by others!

Though slavery and colonialism were gone, their perpetrators, Westerners, were still seen as Africa's enemies. Somehow, despite Western education and christianity, the West was perceived as hostile. The Soviet Union, the embodiment of the East to us, was seen as a savior. There was the general perception that the corrupt politicians and rich exploiters were supported by the West. After all, they kept their stolen money in Swiss banks. The workers and the common people sought the assistance of socialist countries. It was the Eastern bloc that cared for the have-nots, because their workers ruled and knew the problems of the working class and the disadvantaged. Leaders like Nikita Khrushchev, Josip Broz Tito, and Mao Zedong were impressed upon people's minds. Scholarships from Bulgaria, Yugoslavia, China, and the USSR lured many students of my generation abroad.

By the 1970s socialism had a firm grip on the minds of the young African intellectuals. I can recollect clearly the pandemonium that erupted at the 1977 Ibadan conference on "Radical Perspectives in African literature." There was a fistfight as young radicals attacked the old renegades. I presented a paper in which I questioned the social relevance of J.P. Clark's poetry. Soyinka was attacked for being reactionary for writing about Yoruba myths and traditional rulers—what the radicals termed the "kabiyesi syndrome." The veteran dramatist's *Death and the King's Horseman* was specially targeted for criticism. Of course, Soyinka, who never leaves you with the last word, shot back with the now-famous "Who's Afraid of Elesin Oba?" It was only when the Swedish Academy's Nobel Committee a decade later cited that very same play as a classic that we Africans accepted it for what it rightly is!

By the late 1970s and early 1980s it had become fashionable for many African writers to be socialist. I know colleagues who proclaimed themselves Marxists: Ada Ugah, who wrote *Song of Talakawa*; Niyi Osundare, who wrote *Songs of the Marketplace*; and Festus Iyayi who wrote *Violence*. Ngugi, of course, was of the Soyinka generation but socialist. I myself was socialist in tendency but rejected being an ideologue. Many poems of the "In the Undergrowth" section of *The Eagle's Vision* carry the marks of this socialist phase. Poems such as "The Outcast," "Street Boy Blues," "The Patriots," "The Invitation List," and "I Be Somebody" came out of this phase, in which I ranged with the majority in themes, form, and language. I read Frantz Fanon, Amilcar Cabral, Jean-Paul Sartre, and Terry Eagleton, among others. The message became so important that the poetics of form and expression were played down. I would venture to say that this phase might not have been the most poetic but was certainly the most lively in African literature, save perhaps Negritude. Socialism entered African literature to reinforce the tradition itself and especially the activist role of the verbal artist. It only threw a pattern of haves and have-nots over a conflict which has been created by socio-political issues, particularly the worsening economies of African states, exacerbated by the International Monetary Fund and World Bank conditionalities and structural adjustments.

One of the directions I took in the early 1980s was exposure to other cultures. From 1978 to 1981 I attended Syracuse University in upstate New York, taking an M.A. in creative writing and a Ph.D. in English. George P. Elliott, who supervised my M.A. creative writing thesis, liked Amos Tutuola and wanted me to be a little more fantastical. Philip Booth, another of my poetry teachers and a disciplined craftsman himself, asked why my poems were so short. I was already in the doctoral program when Hayden Carruth came to the department. We have been friends ever since, and he has remained a great mentor to me. He loved Okigbo's poetry and saw immeasurable potential in my own, especially in its ideas, form, and language. He advised me to try the long line and to loosen up, to be lighthearted once in a while. The creative-writing program afforded me the opportunity to meet other poets and to be guided by experienced teachers. I had the time to write, and somehow Syracuse gave me immense confidence that I could become a great poet.

By the time I returned to Nigeria in December 1981, Syl Cheney-Coker, an accomplished Sierra Leonean poet, was in the English Department of the University of Maiduguri, where I had to teach after my graduate fellowship. I was to share the same office with him for three years, and I profited enormously from his company. Cheney-Coker was the first to introduce me to Latin American and Caribbean poets. He had just published his *Graveyard Also Has Teeth* and impressed me as a most ingenious poet. He gave me his personal copies of César Vallejo and Pablo Neruda, and from him I read Caribbean poets either in English or in translation. From my undergraduate days I had known only Léon Damas and Aimé Césaire, the Negritude poets. Cheney-Coker also opened me to European poets in translation, and I will always be grateful for his exposing me to Russian and modern Greek poets as well. I started with Alexander Blok, before going to Boris Pasternak, Osip Mandelstam, Anna Akhmatova, and Marina Tsvetaeva. I was mesmerized by these Russian poets of the early 20th century. Even though I had met Voznesensky in Syracuse, I had not known the wealth of Russian poetry till Cheney-Coker opened my eyes to it . He did the same for modern Greek poetry. Very soon I had copies of Yannis Ritsos, George Seferis, Cavafy, and the great one, Odysseus Elytis. My own poetry would never be the same again after this exposure. I had seen the sublime. Poetry is a human song that, although rooted in an experience, transcends the ordinary.

My experience of gradual exposure to other cultures and their poetry might not have been unique at that time. There has been a movement away from confronting the West and asserting our African culture toward knowing what others outside the English-speaking world are and have been doing in poetry. A crop of well-educated poets, many with doctoral degrees and educated abroad, have started to expand their concept of poetry. The poem may be personal and rooted in African culture and yet not preclude a craft learned from the outside. Rather, paradoxically, as I exposed myself to poetry from other cultures and especially from the non-English world, I was researching Urhobo folklore. In 1976 and 1977 in particular, I collected and translated many *udje* dance songs from the Ujevwe and Udu areas. *Udje* songs are mainly satires and dirges. In its heyday in the 1940s and 1950s *udje* dance spread to most parts of Urhobo. Experts were recruited to teach the residents of those areas that did not have the tradition. *Udje* dance songs are composed in a workshop. The *ororile*, the poet, collects the materials for the song and presents his composition to the workshop participants to "straighten it out." Later, a sweet-voiced individual is asked to sing the song. This cantor is called an *obo-ile*. Usually fictitious names are given to real characters of the community who have been involved in scandals or have violated the traditional ethos. Although *udje* dance and songs gradually "died" in those areas where they were introduced as something new, they remain strong in Udu, Ujevwe, and parts of eastern Urhobo. In 1977 I met the distinguished Okitiakpe of Ekakpamre, one of the greatest poets I have known. By then he was old and frail, and he asked his eldest daughter to sing his songs to me. He was to die several years later while I was abroad. *Udje* taught me much about the Urhobo philosophy of life and literary aesthetics. My research into *udje* dance songs and songs by notable Urhobo artists such as Ogute and Omokomoko has opened me to the immense poetry of my people. I will continue to acknowledge my indebtedness to these great traditional Urhobo artists, from whom I learned how to sing.

My forays into my native poetic forms were part of a general trend. As Soyinka and Clark had earlier delved into Yoruba and Urhobo/Ijo dramatic and poetic forms respectively, so would poets of my generation all over Africa explore their linguistic and cultural heritage. Niyi Osundare looked into Yoruba, Kofi Anyidoho into Ewe, and Jack Mapanje into Chewa. Unlike the Soyinka-generation poets who exposed the material culture through mainly Western poetic techniques, my coevals seem to have been more interested in the poetic forms and techniques of our own cultures for expressing our experiences.

The interest in indigenous poetic forms leads me to the use of language. In my undergraduate years, the language debate in African literature had abated without resolution. Many writers had made their choices on whether to use African or European languages in their writings. By the early 1980s Ngugi had resolved to use Gikuyu rather than English. I have attempted some poems in Urhobo and a few in pidgin English, but have decided for now to write in English. I realize that the ideal thing is for me to write in the language of my culture. However, the allegiance of many Africans has been stretched beyond the local language group. I am a Nigerian, an African, and a human being. I want to reach Nigerians, Africans, and all humanity. My images, symbols, and references deriving from Urhobo folklore give a distinctive tone to my poetry. Thus, though I write in English, I try to infuse my verse with fresh nuances and rhythms that I carry from the Urhobo language. I may be writing in English, but it is not quite the same English as the British or the Americans or Australians write. I have endeavored to Africanize the language to serve my ends.

Sometime in the 1970s and between 1982 and about 1985 I was interested in the mystical. For my personal development and discipline, I sought mystical knowledge. Raised in a supernatural environment, I considered such pursuit of the mystical to be normal. That pursuit did not seek indigenous mysticism, however, but rather mysticism from books. I read about ancient Egypt, the Rosicrucians, Tibet, and Lobsang Rampa. A poem like "Under My Skin" in *Labyrinths of the Delta* could only have come from this inner quest.

The mid-1980s were for my generation what the early 1960s were for the Soyinka group of Lenrie Peters, Kofi Awoonor, Okigbo, Clark, and Brutus: excitement. Soyinka's Nobel Prize for Literature in 1986 gave all of us a great lift toward what is achievable. This together with other smaller prizes that others and I won gave us confidence to sing more. The reception arranged for me after my receipt of the Commonwealth Poetry Prize for the Africa Region in 1988 and other honors gave me a sense of responsibility. The 1980s saw the proliferation of poetry workshops in many African universities: Maiduguri, Zaria, Ibadan, Nsukka, Legon (Ghana), and Zomba (Malawi), among others. There was no limit to our achievement, which itself was our hope in our future.

However, things were to change fast and drastically. The gains of the 1970s and early 1980s were evaporating due to the harsh economic situations in most African states. Publishing avenues were diminishing; poetry magazines and literary journals such as *Okike* and *Black Orpheus* became dormant. By the late 1980s African writers were singing dirges for the continent. The poetry, according to a colleague, had become that of the stomach. Another generation of younger, less well educated writers were at our heels. Money is very important to them. Suffering has taught them to go for remuneration by any means necessary. Despite this anger and depression, however, poetry will not die. Poetry is an immortal goddess who will continue to be worshiped for as long as there is life.

Now that I am in my forties and away from home, I am attempting to see with a third eye and experience life with a sixth sense. It is not just political corruption that interests me. I probe into the psyches of human beings to find what makes them different. My love cannot be as uninhibited as it used to to be. Married now, with children, I am in many ways no longer a free person. I have deeper philosophical and cultural concerns. Though I am still learning from life, as everyone continues to do till the end, I can speak with some experience, especially of my time. I have seen hopes and expectations rise, only to be shattered by the lack of leadership. Now I do not blame the leaders alone. In "Why Should We Not Die?" I have blamed the ruler and the ruled.

> First came rinderpest.
> The vegetarians in our midst didn't care
> about the killer of cows.
> Then came locusts and drought,
> and the night fell upon all.
> The people blamed it on the head,
> the head blamed it on the people;
> they didn't believe in shared responsibility.

There is so much the rulers and the ruled might have borne with love.

Once a colleague asked me to tell my love history. I was shaken by the question, as I never expected my love history to be publicized. My relatives and friends have appeared in my poems. I will never forget my grandmother, who did not live to see me beyond my undergraduate years. As for my late father, I wrote: "Since you left, / I have been re-painting you / in my closet / with brighter and smoother colours. / I see fresh facets, invisible / in your lifetime." I have had a friend who will remain an angel in the plateau of my mind. I have used *Ita*, the Hausa word for "She," as her fictional name. Several of my poems are tributes to those I love.

Currently, I am looking at poetry in the larger social, cultural, and political context. I have just completed a manuscript titled *The Day-dream of Ants* on the impact of modern technology on contemporary African lives: the comfort and convenience of cars, planes, birth control pills, condoms, et cetera, in an African environment. I go back to Africa very often to reconnect with home. By my last visit it has become com-mon to find CNN International there and so current—this among a non-literate people accustomed to using only memory for storing their folklore. Everything is being computerized. The African soul is in peril of losing its identity. The influences of Americanization, Europeaniza-tion, Westernization and Islamization run so deep that we risk being ab-sorbed in the Westernization/Americanization of the globe.

My work in progress focuses on traditional African institutions, philosophies, and practices commemorated in artworks that can inspire contemporary Africans to overcome their obstacles. Africans today ap-pear helplessly overwhelmed by a plethora of problems. These are of such magnitude that many people are hopelessly resigned to accepting them as part of normal human experience. Tradition and memory tell that Africans had faced life-threatening difficulties in the past and drawn from their inner selves the resources with which to combat those adversities successfully. Coincidentally, most of these institutions, prac-tices, and philosophies have been preserved in one type of art or other. I am interested in writing poems on these mainly visual artworks, which reflect traditional ideas that are ignored at the peril of contempo-rary Africans. The Shona *mbira* is not just an instrument but the power within it which transcends the realm of the physical world to represent the power to translate wishes into reality. The *Ivwri* was used by the Urhobo to defend themselves during the slave-trade period. Another Urhobo concept is that of *Ivwie*, the cry for justice, a most relevant theme in contemporary Africa. I have written on all these, and to re-mind contemporary African leaders of a tradition of responsible gover-nance, I am currently writing on *Edon*, where would-be rulers learned the dos and don'ts of leadership. I have also written on the Igbo *mbari* and *ikenga*.

At this stage I feel that condemnation and lamentation are not enough for the African. I believe that commemoration of all that is good in the past and is still viable but ignored in the present should inspire hope. We need not write dirges for the living. For me there is hope, and that should be the common pursuit of African writers. We should be builders. Our vision should be such that will raise us from the current low state to high hopes of what we can be.

I have been a witness to and a chronicler of my time. One cannot live outside one's time, even if one projects oneself into times future or past. Attempting to see beneath the surface is what I strive to do. I want to be an oracle, a knower of hidden things, the knower of the other side of things; not a conventional oracle who foresees doom, but the oracle of good tidings, the oracle who alerts his people against taking a course that leads to doom. The things we need to do to overturn current hardships are there for us to seize upon. One finger has to point out those things that need to be done. That's the sort of poet I would like to be known as. The poet should be an oracle and a healer. All the more reason that our vision should be one of hope: for restoration of the good we have lost, for attainment of a state of well-being. Only hope can save us.

10

Poetic Imagination in Black Africa

The poet in black Africa has a distinctive character that is derived from his literary traditions and sense of mission. Although modern African literature is written in a foreign language (English, French, or Portuguese), it strongly mirrors traditional indigenous cultures. In addition, it is marked by teaching and satire. The conditions of the age have also placed their stamp on the African imagination, producing types of poetry that seem to characterize developing societies.

In Africa a poet is not only a specially gifted person but also a gauge of his society's condition. More perceptive than the man of common disposition, he sees through the surface of things, through what appears to the rest of society as opaque. Lenrie Peters, the Gambian poet, knows the "lies behind the truth" (19). To the Nigerian Christopher Okigbo,

who could jump your eye,
your mind-window,

And I said:
The prophet only the poet   (9).

In other words, the poet and the prophet are the same in that both possess the quality of insight. Doubtless it was the heightened qualities of prophecy, foresight, and insight that enabled Okigbo to prophesy the Nigerian crisis of the late sixties. In "Come Thunder" he foresees the chaos which preceded the army take-over in 1966:

Now that the triumphant march has entered
    the last street corners,
Remember, O dancers, the thunder among the clouds...
Now that laughter, broken in two, hangs tremulous
    between the teeth,
Remember, O dancers, the lightning beyond the earth...
The smell of blood already floats in the lavender-
    mist of the afternoon.
The death sentence lies in ambush along the
    corridor of power;
And a great fearful thing already tugs at the
    cables of the open air,

A nebula immense and immeasurable, a night
    of deep waters—
An iron dream unnamed and unprintable, a path
    of stone   (66).

The poet's foresight is reinforced by his personal experience, for

The drowsy heads of the pods in barren farmlands
    witness it,
The homesteads abandoned in this country's brush
    fire witness it:
The myriad eyes of deserted corn cobs in burning barns
    witness it   (66).

The inner vision of the poet gives him an advantage in society. J.P. Clark assumes special insight in "What the Squirrel Said," a poem about the January 1966 coup in Nigeria:

THEY KILLED the lion in his den
But left the leopard to his goats
They killed the bull without horns
But left the crocodile to litter the field
They killed a sheep who played the shepherd
But left the hyrax who was hyena   (13).

Since the poet in Africa holds himself high relative to the rest of his society, he appears to be proud. In 1962 Okigbo boasted in Kampala, Uganda, that he did not read his poetry to non-poets. The Olympian Wole Soyinka remains distant from the society he tries to enlighten. Lenrie Peters's learning elevates him to a pedestal higher than his African audience can easily reach. Most of the eminent poets in Africa—Clark, Okigbo, Peters, Soyinka, Taban lo Liyong, and Okot p'Bitek—exhibit common traits and similar ideas about the vocation of literature. They conceive themselves to be sages who possess deep wisdom, wide knowledge, and large experience. Seeing through superficial phenomena, they tend to observe and dramatize the irony of things.

Many African poets regard themselves as cultural standard-bearers charged with a peculiar sense of mission. The Ghanaian Kofi Awoonor is a bard of the Anlo Ewe, the Nigerian Soyinka has his mentor Ogun, the Yoruba god of hunters and craftsmen; Okigbo asks for poetic inspiration from "mother Idoto." I myself rely on Uhaghwa, the Urhobo god of songs. A poet fortunate enough to speak for people who have a traditional and ancient culture shares in an environment which is not merely geographical and historical but also psychological, conveying a highly charged state of mind.

Many of these poets employ the rituals, myths, legends, beliefs, world-view, and history of their peoples to express their ideas. Soyinka's "Dedication" is a ritual in which the speaker projects the positive qualities of the earth and its fauna and flora into a newly born girl so that she will live a safe, fruitful, and long life:

> ...child, palm oil on your tongue
>
> Is suppleness to life, and wine of this gourd
> From self-same timeless run of runnels as refill
> Your podlings, child, weaned from yours we embrace
>
> Earth's honeyed milk, wine of the only rib.
> Now roll your tongue in honey till your cheeks are
> Swarming honeycombs—your world needs sweetening, child
>
> Camwood round the heart, chalk for flight
> Of blemish—see? it dawns!—antimony beneath
> Armpits like a goddess, and leave this taste
>
> Long on your lips, of salt, that you may seek
> None from tears. This, rain-water, is the gift
> Of gods—drink of its purity, bear fruits in season.
>
> Fruits then to your lips: haste to repay
> The debt of birth. Yield man-tides like the sea
> And ebbing, leave a meaning on the fossilled sands
>
> (*Idanre*, 24–25).

The poem is a rendition of the Yoruba christening ceremony. The emphasis of the poem is on the triple desires in the Yoruba value system: children, wealth, and long life. This poem is the African counterpart of Yeats's "Prayer for My Daughter." The poetic expression is highly indebted to the Yoruba language of the poet.

Like Soyinka, Okot p'Bitek draws on African traditions. He employs the Acoli culture of Uganda as the vehicle of his critique of modern African urban society in *Song of Lawino* and *Song of Ocol*. Clark, in "Ivbie," absorbs Urhobo and Ijo cultures of the Delta area of Nigeria to condemn imperialism and colonialism. Oswald Mtshali appears to be the modern Zulu standard-bearer as he celebrates the birth of Shaka in *Sounds of a Cowhide Drum*. Even the much-acclaimed Gambian internationalist Lenrie Peters could not resist the African cultural charm in "Katchikali." The indebtedness to the indigenous culture is such that the poets seem to be translating from local languages into English when they use African proverbs. Okigbo says in "Hurrah for Thunder,"

> The eye that looks down will surely see the nose;
> The finger that fits should be used to pick the nose   (67).

Soyinka has a wealth of proverbial sayings in *Ogun Abibiman*:

> In time of race, no beauty slights the duiker's
> In time of strength, the elephant stands alone
> In time of hunt, the lion's grace is holy
> In time of flight, the egret mocks the envious
> In time of strife, none vies with Him
> Of seven paths, Ogun...   (7).

Proverbs give African poetry a certain peculiarity of expression which distinguishes it from poetry elsewhere.

African cultural consciousness is also very intense in Léopold Senghor, Birago Diop, and other poets with a strong sense of black awareness, who tend to romanticize ancient Africa. By embracing their ethnic cultures, these writers show that their origins as men and their impulse and power as artists are inseparable. Thus they propagate their minicultures in their work. They also realize that most of their public shares with them the same traditional background, and that cultural references serve as exotic spices to readers.

The poet's conception of himself as more perceptive and sensitive than the ordinary person in his society encourages him to assume a didactic role. This role originates in the tradition of teaching with folktales and songs. To be a credible teacher, the poet assumes a traditional African role—sage, priest, prophet, or even a god's representative on earth. Soyinka, for instance, conveys the impression that he is the mundane equivalent of Ogun, the dual-natured Yoruba god.

Having presented himself as a qualified teacher, the African poet reports something to his people. He rarely describes for the sake of merely describing. Didacticism, not lyricism, prevails in modern African poetry. Ideas rather than feelings are emphasized. As Ali Mazrui puts it, African poetry in the traditional mode is "emphatically an exercise in *meaning*. There are themes to follow; tales to tell" (47).

There is in African poetry a crisis atmosphere in which the poet is a savior who wants to deliver an urgent message. Okigbo was urgent as he prophesied political trouble in Nigeria. In "Hurrah for Thunder," he says:

> If I don't learn to shut my mouth I'll soon go to hell
> I, Okigbo, town-crier, together with my iron bell   (67).

The poet here is the crier who alerts his society about what is happening or is about to happen.

Peters is perhaps the African poet most zealously determined to instruct his readers. In *Satellites*, he says:

I want to
drag you out
shake your eyes
open with pictures
sounds and words
compel your imagination

Drag you to
your knees till
you sniff the
throwback of
my vision
with ease   (18).

Like a preacher, he tells his audience:

To reach God
Man must transcend
the present moment
Exchange knowledge of self
for that of others
Desisting immediacy
only with intimacy
of universal distress.
To reach God
Man must be worthy
of His image   (61).

Peters uses rhetoric to convey his vision of things to his audience. He
speaks clearly and repeats. His syntax is lucid, and his words are exact,
not ambiguous.

The traditional teaching role of the African poet has been heightened
in modern times. Highly educated poets feel obliged to enlighten their
people and readers, since in many African societies the literacy rate and
socio-political consciousness are very low. Because of the didactic incli-
nation of the African imagination, there is interest in socio-political criticism manifested in satire and ideological commitment. Satire, like
teaching, is in the African poetic vein. The poets assail the negative
forces in their respective societies in order to bring about improve-
ments. Okot p'Bitek makes fun of the cultural copycats of Ugandan society, who embrace Western cultural modes without leaving room for
their African heritage. Lawino pokes fun at Clementine and Ocol, the
cultural renegades of Acoli society. In a similar manner, Oswald Mtshali in "The Detribalized" ridicules those Africans who become cultural bastards in order to be considered civilized.

Soyinka satirizes the military leaders of Nigeria in *A Shuttle in the Crypt*. He indicts the military establishment for its hypocrisy, tyranny, and inhumanity, indirectly asking for a humane, virtuous, and free society. The African poet is a defender of the positive values of his society, not just a teacher. Soyinka, like the god Ogun, is an "orphans' shield," a defender of the helpless.

The problems in Africa put the writer in a position of choice—for or against. Good is pitched against evil, as in the vatic tradition. To a large extent, African writers are committed in varying degrees. G-C. Mutiso has this to say of them:

> In their expression of preferences for certain outcomes over others, the writers are acting within their roles as recorders, interpreters and especially judges of the society of which they are a part. To the extent that they offer choices and criticisms of social phenomena, their ideas have a clear social and political relevance. All literature in the African context tends to function as a kind of social commentary. The artist creates art based on the ideas and problems which exist in his own particular society (7).

African poets are artists in the Orwellian sense, since they seem to write with "a desire to push the world in a certain direction, to alter other people's idea of the type of society that they should strive after (Mutiso 4). Soyinka, for example, looks toward an idyllic and agrarian society. Peters is not alone as a dreamer.

The poet's special gift and his didactic role enable him to assume the responsibility of spokesman for the black race. This feature of African imagination is an extension of the communal solidarity in folk songs. The assertion of blackness or black solidarity is not solely the preoccupation of francophone African writers. Soyinka, who attacks negritude in his London poems, *Ogun Abibiman*, and in the much quoted statement, "a tiger does not proclaim its tigritude, but it pounces," is as aware of the African cultural heritage as Senghor or David Diop. Clark and Soyinka are spokesmen for the black race in "Ivbie" and *Ogun Abibiman* respectively. In "Ivbie," Clark catalogues the exploitation of Africa by colonialists, a theme strongly expressed by the Senegalese David Diop in "Afrique" and other poems. Soyinka has the double function of encouraging black liberation fighters in South Africa and defending violence as a just means of achieving black rights and independence after the failure of diplomatic and peaceful attempts.

The solidarity of black peoples expressed in African poetry arises from the historical heritage the writers share. This sense of racial unity travels across oceans and is discernible in the writing of blacks from the Caribbean, the United States, and South America. In dealing with black solidarity, poets tend to correct prejudicial impressions of foreigners about Africa. Soyinka does this:

> ...Vengeance
> is not the god we celebrate, nor hate,
> Nor blindness to the loss that follows
> In His wake.
> Nor ignorance of history's bitter reckoning
> On innocent alike. Our songs acclaim
> Cessation of a long despair, extol the ends
> Of sacrifice born in our will, not weakness   (20–21).

There is a strong sense of history in African poetry. The great issues are slavery, colonialism, culture conflict, civil war, apartheid, post-independence frustration, and neocolonialism. The current trend of harsh irony in literary works is related to the poets' perception of African rulers as falling short of their social and political ideals. The caustic dialogue between a subject and a ruler in Peters's "In the beginning" illustrates this point:

> 'I see
> But my children—
> beg pardon Sir,
> will they go to school?'
> Later!
> 'Will they have food to eat
> and clothes to wear?'
> Later I tell you!
> 'Beg pardon Sir;
> a house like yours?'
> Put this man in jail   (84).

Because the poet satirizes repressive forces and is committed to progress, he tends to be a victim—of society, political rulers, or destiny. The victim figure is pervasive. The poet's society makes fun of him as a dreamer, like Peters; rulers persecute him for outspokenness, as they have persecuted Soyinka, Dennis Brutus, and Mtshali. Besides, destiny subjects him to the natural laws of age and death, like every human being. The poet always tends to have something to complain about, hence the maudlin tone. Despite his gifts of foresight and learning, he is low in the social scheme and an outsider to decision-making. These realities often give him authority to speak for the masses and attack the rulers. During the Nigerian crisis, for example, Soyinka spoke for the suffering Igbo people.

The African poet also has a private life which gives uniqueness to his writing. Clark in "For Granny (from Hospital)" recollects

> ...the loud note of quarrels
> And endless dark nights of intrigue
> In Father's house of many wives   (*A Reed in the Tide*, 1).

Nostalgia is a common feature, especially noticeable in the early edition of Okigbo's *Heavensgate*. The bulk of Soyinka's *A Shuttle in the Crypt*, Awoonor's *Ride Me, Memory*, Clark's *Casualties*, and Brutus's *Letters to Martha and Other Poems from a South African Prison* are exhumed experiences.

Despite the tendencies of African poets toward social criticism, commitment, and spokesmanship for the people and the black race, there are variations. The Cameroonian Mbella Sonne Dipoko, author of *Black and White in Love*, feels that the poet should be totally disengaged from politics and its prejudices; hence he avoids politics in his poetry. To Soyinka, however, "the man dies in all who keep silent in the face of tyranny" (1975, 13). His vision, shown in *The Man Died* and *A Shuttle in the Crypt,* is not acceptable to the establishment.

Some writers do not fit into an African mold. The poetic imagination is, of course, not uniform; nor can imagination be unitary or collective because of diverse individual experiences and the influences of different geographical areas. Though African poets emphasize the meaning of ideas, some writers are inevitably obscure. Ali Mazrui links obscurity in African poetry with "Protestantism and...liberal individualism" (47). Those who practice obscurity are abstract—especially the Nigerian Okigbo and Soyinka, who display modernist tendencies in their fragmentation, incoherent images, and disconnected thought. Mazrui considers "abstract exercises with verbal pictures...a profound departure from the tradition" because of the learning evident in such work (48).

Some of these poetic qualities, along with their variations and deviations, are not unique to Africa. The poet, wherever he is, draws ideas from a common cosmic pool. Besides, the modern world is so cosmopolitan that there is no literary island not influenced by the rest of the world. Human problems also tend to be universal—corruption, tyranny, love, death, and so forth. For example, Soyinka in *The Man Died* and *A Shuttle in the Crypt* is aiming not only at social criticism but also at recording as a witness the atrocities of Nigerian military leaders—much as Mandelstam and Solzhenitsyn have done in exposing the shortcomings of the Soviet system. The poet—whether in the Soviet Union, Africa, or South America—will continue to revolt against injustice, lack of freedom, oppression, and exploitation as long as those problems prevail in his environment.

The volksgeist affects the poetry of a particular region at certain times of its history in the move from traditionalism to modernity and from underdevelopment to development. Some of the social problems that concern certain African poets have preoccupied and continue to preoccupy many South American writers. César Vallejo and Pablo Neruda were social critics in their own ways. Critical and historical concerns are therefore not unique to the modern African imagination.

Despite its closeness to some other literatures, African poetry is different from its American counterpart. Poets in the United States do not see the need to teach because of the high degree of enlightenment in their society. Rarely is there any social criticism in contemporary American poetry. Aggressive individualism and a measure of material well-being seem to have made the American poet turn inward. While Lenrie Peters is interested in the physical welfare of the masses and the availability of schools, and Okot p'Bitek is concerned with the type of government his country adopts, the contemporary American poet is not his brother's keeper or his society's savior. He shows a certain indifference toward politics. Ezra Pound was a single voice in his time; the Beat Generation writers who criticized the establishment were outside the American mainstream. Despite the civil rights movement and the Vietnam war, the personal problems of confessional poets have become the vogue in America.

The African poetic imagination, on the other hand, draws on individual experiences as well as shared culture, environment, and history. Nourished by special roots, the poet in Africa assumes the responsibility of teaching and fighting verbally to save his people.

Works Cited

Awoonor, Kofi. *Ride Me, Memory*. Greenfield Center, NY: Greenfield Review Press, 1973.

Brutus, Dennis. *Letters to Martha and Other Poems from a South African Prison*. London: Heinemann, 1971.

Clark, J.P. *A Reed in the Tide*. London: Longman, 1965.

———. *Casualties*. London: Longman, 1971.

Dipoko, Mbella Sonne. *Black & White in Love*. London: Heinemann, 1972.

Lo Liyong, Taban. *Frantz Fanon's Uneven Ribs*. London: Heinemann, 1971.

Mazrui, Ali. "Abstract Verse and African Tradition." *Zuka* 1 (Sept. 1967).

Moore, Gerald and Ulli Beier. eds. *Modern Poetry from Africa*. Harmondsworth, England: Penguin, 1967.

Mtshali, Oswald. *Sounds of a Cowhide Drum*. Oxford: OUP, 1978.

Mutiso, G-C. *Socio-political Thought in African Literature*. London: Macmillan, 1974.

Ojaide, Tanure. *Children of Iroko & Other Poems*. Greenfield Center, NY: Greenfield Review Press, 1973.

Okigbo, Christopher. *Labyrinths*. London: Heinemann, 1971.

p'Bitek, Okot. *Song of Lawino*. Nairobi: EAPH, 1966.

———. *Song of Ocol*. Nairobi: EAPH, 1967.

Peters, Lenrie. *Satellites*. London: Heinemann, 1967.

———. *Katchikali*. London: Heinemann, 1971.

Soyinka, Wole. *Idanre and Other Poems*. London: Eyre Methuen, 1967.

———. *A Shuttle in the Crypt*. London: Rex Collings/Methuen, 1972.

———. *The Man Died*. Harmondsworth, England: Penguin, 1975.

———. *Ogun Abibiman*. London: Rex Collings, 1978.

Index